Houseplants
and indoor landscaping

otography...
Arthur Orans

cknowledgments

C. Kind Florist, New York City, who per-
ed use of his large collection of color illustra-
s. Also, to the following for allowing Arthur
Orans to photograph plants necessary for
nding out the collection contained herein:
oklyn Botanic Garden, Flowertime of Hun-
ton, The Greenhouse, Henry Herb LA, Mid-
d Nursery, National Maritime Union, Ott's
enhouses, Vosters Greenhouses and Leslie
el. Thanks must be extended to those firms
associations that permitted us to use pic-
s showing plantlife effectively utilized in
e interiors.

ur Cover

indoor landscape and its east window
ain of compatible, trailing tropical plants
transformed the combination kitchen and
ng area of this New Hope, Pennsylvania
e into a year-round garden. — Courtesy
tkote Flooring Products

B. Morse Countryside Publications, A.B.
rse Division of the Barrington Press. Copy-
nt © 1973 by the A. B. Morse Co., 200 James
, Barrington, Ill. 60010.

P/BN 5033

Table of Contents

About the Author

Muriel Orans is a widely published writer. Her articles have appeared in many trade magazines, professional journals and newspapers, including the New York and London Times. Writing has been a natural adjunct to a hobby of growing indoor and outdoor plants from the time she was eight years of age.

Mrs. Orans was a prime force in organization of the Indoor Light Gardening Society. She also has been active in the American Horticultural Society, International Geranium Society and Association for the Advancement of Science. The Federated Garden Clubs, through two chapters, utilized Mrs. Orans to head up district youth programs.

Her interest in youth spilled over into New York City public schools as industry coordinator for school gardening. Mrs. Orans served in this capacity during the 1960's. Work pioneered in New York now is being copied in other metropolitan areas across the U.S.

Another facet of Mrs. Orans' gardening interest has been research. In 1960 she became a consultant to Brookhaven National Laboratories. During the same year her "Crookneck Report" was published in the Penn State Geranium Manual. She presently is working on a selection of indoor plant materials that the novice may grow successfully. Much of what she has learned is contained within the pages of this book.

International Standard Book Number 0-88453- 000-0

Library of Congress Catalog Card Number: 73:88247

Third printing February, 1975

Introduction

You can grow attractive, decorative plants indoors with a minimum amount of effort or knowhow. Producing perfect specimens, while commendable, is practical only if the grower is prepared to reproduce these plants' native environments. However, for happy indoor gardening, be content if your plants retain much of their form, texture, habit and color that first attracted you to them.

All plants discussed here are proven performers for indoor growers in average environmental situations. All are available from garden centers, plant boutiques, florists, pot plant shops, supermarkets, dime stores and many via air mail.

Without light there is no life. The plants are listed according to the amount of available light required for growth, even though it may not be the optimum amount. Other factors such as temperature, humidity, air circulation, traffic and compatibility will all fall into place so that your plants will adjust, adapt, acclimate, tolerate, thrive or survive without your having to

make many changes to meet t cultural needs.

Achieving perfection is an excell goal for any project, but in the cas growing plants for enjoyment, bother unless you are entering ther competition.

Who takes home blue ribbons a flower show? Rarely the window gardener because it's impossible produce the enormous floriferous, rounded, colorful products that greenhouse grower displays. Ot winners also include the serious h byist who, if he grows at the windo deepens his shelves by building out attaching racks to give his plants space they require for perfection a the artificial light gardener who inv in special lighting equipment, tim misters, self-waterers, humidifiers,

I've gone all the aforemention routes; earned my blue ribbons a Award of Merit in horticulture, bu can honestly state that I am hap now, gardening for my own satisfact than when preparing plants for com tition.

By selecting the plants I grow to according to the light available, years of experience, love and obser tion are rewarding me with heal thriving plants that receive a minim of care.

They may not be perfect specim seen at shows, but I'm satisfied and are my parakeets that fly freely amo them and nibble the fresh greens will. Also appreciative are people pass by my street-side windows wh even in mid-winter they can en petunias and geraniums bloom among pineapple plants, the fla foliage of Rex Begonias and fragr wild growth of cooking herbs wh growth can only be kept in bounds frequent clipping.

You too can be a successful ind gardener if you select your plants matching their light requirements the kind of light you have to of Compatability and other conside tions will follow.

elect Plants Wisely

With so many plant outlets avail-
ble, word of mouth recommendations
e probably best for selecting a reli-
ble vendor. If this is not possible, seek
store or garden center that specializes
potted plants, preferably someone
ho has been doing business at the
me location for at least two years.
his is especially important if you plan
purchase a large, expensive, decor-
or specimen.

A reliable vendor will offer large
ants that have been hardened off and
climated to average interior growing
nditions. This is done by holding
wly-arrived field stock grown in
orida and Puerto Rico for at least a
onth in a shady, cool location such as
greenhouse or modified light
amber. Some northern growers and
ower-vendors will even repot the
ants, using a more suitable soil mix.
pest control program also is insti-
ted at this time to destroy infesta-
ns that escape the eyes of USDA in-
ectors, who check all agricultural
oducts moving interstate or coming
to the U.S. from another country.

Very satisfactory material can be
btained via mail order, if certain
naller plants desired are not available
cally. These have been inspected
rior to packaging and shipment for
isease and pests.

Choose your plants as you would
ble fruits and vegetables. They
ould be bursting with health, exhi-
iting rich color, unblemished foliage,
nd compact growth.

Avoid spindly, leggy plants, unless
ey are typical of their variety. Also
void plants with yellowing, blotched
r otherwise abnormal foliage. These
roblems indicate poor cultural
nanagement and/or pest infestation.
a plant is staked, make sure that the
lant is being supported. Often, stakes
ide stem cracks or breaks.

Carefully inspect plants for pests
nder leaves, particularly at their axils
nd on woody parts of the plant. Avoid
nose that manifest signs of insect in-
station such as miniscule red dots or

tiny webs under the leaves (red spider),
small cotton puffs found at leaf axils
(mealy bugs), dandruff-like flakes
under leaves that fly in swarms when
disturbed (white fly), or hard-shelled
insects that look like mini-oyster shells
on bark or leaves of glossy varieties
(scale).

Uninvited guests of this sort are un-
necessary and diminish pleasure
gained from new specimens.

Store-Home Precautions

Newly-purchased plants must be
wrapped even if they will only have to
be carried next door. They need this
protection to cut down on root disturbance and to serve as insulation
against high temperature, rapid drying
and freezing.

Plants, like man, consist mainly of
water. A few minutes exposure to
freezing temperatures is enough to
cause ice crystals to form in the leaves,
resulting in their destruction and pos-
sibly death to the plant.

No matter how pest-free and clean
your new plants appear, do not be in a
rush to place them among existing ones
in your collection. Rather, place them
in a shady, temperate location away
from the rest. In this manner the new
plants will have a chance to adjust to
their new environment, yet have
enough time to hatch out any uninvited
guests. A quarantine of at least a week
will serve both purposes.

If all the plants remain pest-free, you
can place them among others. If even
one plant is infected, hold them all in
isolation until the problem is controlled or the plants are discarded.

Preparations for receipt of mailorder
plants should be made ahead of time.
Have soil, pots, space, etc., prepared so
little time will be wasted in their
handling. The more quickly plants can
be settled, recovery from travel, lack of
light and potting up will be shortened.

Follow the same procedure illustrated in the "How to Repot" section
with one difference: Jiffy-7 grown
plants (See plants from seeds) should

have the protective net removed. Give
these plants a 3-day recuperative
period and then put them out with the
rest of your plants.

If you are unable to handle new
plants immediately after receipt, open
the shipping box, remove all wrappings
around the plants and give them long
periods of diffused light. Mist if they
appear to be dry.

Water Plants Properly

No plant, unless it is a bog plant
such as cyperus, is happy in a constantly soggy soil or when the soil
moisture content reads halfway down
from the top and a quarter of the way
up from the bottom of the dipstick.
The dry area remaining contributes to
poor root development and resulting
weak plants. Improper watering is the
cause of most plant ills from root rot to
edema and leaf wilt to leaf loss.

Soil has to breathe. In fact, a good
growing soil may consist of 50 per cent
air. Therefore, soil must be permitted a
certain amount of drying out between
waterings to let the air into it.

Amount and frequency of watering
can only be determined by the kinds of
plants grown, the environment and soil
medium. Also contributing to amount
and frequency are the kinds of pots
utilized. Plastic, clay, glazed and un-
glazed containers retain moisture dif-
ferently.

Because every situation is different, I
have devised a simple method to serve
as a guide for just about every kind of
plant that is available today. This is the
"Dipstick," which acts as a simple soil
moisture indicator. Materials available
for use in this manner are countless. It
may be a stick found in the garden, a
plant marker or even a plastic straw
that is slipped between the soil and the
growing pot wall. Whatever is used
must be long enough to reach the bottom of the pot, yet extend an inch or
two above soil level for easy gripping.
When you think plants need watering,
slip out the stick and note how far up
from the bottom to the soil line it is
moist. Watering recommendations for

3

the plants I've listed in this book are described in this manner.

The only answer to "How much?" is "Thoroughly." This means that using luke warm water, pour water in from the top and also set the pot in a water-filled growing saucer. If this water is absorbed within five minutes, repeat the procedure until movement ceases. Let plants sit for an hour, then remove the excess, either by pouring or siphoning.

A handy gadget for siphoning is the turkey baster. This permits access to plants in an indoor landscape situation or when they're double potted in decorator ceramics. Where plants are double-potted, evaporation rate is slowed, thereby cutting down on watering frequency. On the other hand, hanging basket plants may need to be watered daily. Continuous air circulation increases the rate of evaporation.

In a blind watering situation, you will have the aid of the dipstick, but until a plant's water needs have been determined, caution should be exercised. Blind watering is a condition whereby a large tubbed plant is double potted into a decorative ceramic that is much larger than the growing tub. Pebbles and peatmoss are used to fill in bottom and sides of the outer container so that the growing pot stands high enough to reach up to the lip of the outer tub. The surface of both outer and inner containers is top dressed with pebbles, redwood chips or sheet moss.

Remove the dip stick and starting with a quart of water, begin to water-in. Wait a few minutes until all water is absorbed and then measure with a dip stick. Repeat the process until water reaches to the bottom of the outer ceramic, yet not up as high as bottom of growing pot.

When you water terrariums, use a mister, because soil erosion can be a problem. A dipstick slipped into the center will serve as your guide as to when and how much.

Hanging baskets should be brought to the sink for a thorough soaking and to avoid dripping on floors. Double

potting helps to cut down on watering frequency and also serves as a humidifier if the growing pot can sit on a layer of pebbles just about the waterline. Here, too, your dipstick will serve as a guide.

If at any time you think that the top soil feels too dry, yet the dipstick negates your observation, a light water misting may serve as a freshener.

Use Sterilized Soil

You will note that for each plant discussed, I've indicated what indoor growing medium promotes good growth. Most are highly moisture retentive, yet light enough to permit aeration so necessary for good plant health.

An all-purpose sterilized potting soil is a good base for whatever soil mix is desired. Philodendrons, african violets, cactus and succulents all seem to thrive when peatmoss or parakeet gravel is mixed with the potting soil according to these plants' needs.

As with large commercial growers who have gone to this kind of soil program or even to artificial mediums such as Jiffy-mix, I have found results to be consistently good

Houseplanting Tools

Other than a long-necked, thin spout watering can that is light enough for you to handle when filled, all of your basic tools can be found around the house. A Windex spray bottle makes a good plant mister and

tweezers can thin out seedlings. Yo can water unreachable plants with turkey baster without moving any. you overwater, it serves as a siphon remove the excess. Popsicle stick make fine dipsticks, especially in pots inches or less in depth. Straws also ca be used as siphons, dipsticks and ino ganic supports for plant marker flag

Plant marker flags are cut dow index cards stapled to a plastic straw Scissors are for pruning and growing the knife is used for easing the plan out of its container during trans planting. Forks can aerate the soil the top becomes compacted or crusted

The pencil can punch holes suitabl for planting seedlings and the spoo can be utilized for fill-in chores aroun the pot's sides and for top dressing

Which Fertilizer Best?

Forget most of what you've hear about fertilizer. Claims and counter claims by organic and inorganic pro ponents have greatly clouded the issue What you're really interested in is th amount of nitrogen, phosphorus an potassium in the fertilizer. These thre elements, major nutrients, are repre sented on the container by N,P&K. Th numbers in the formula represent th percentage of each element present. A 5-10-5 formula contains 5 per cent ni torgen, 10 per cent phosphorus and per cent potassium. The other 80 pe cent of the formula is inert carrie matter. Other elements in a mix ar usually in trace amounts. A goo houseplant will have many of these ele ments, such as aluminum, boron copper, iron, manganese, molybdenun and zinc present. If there is a price dif ferential between fertilizers with th same formula, you may want to check what trace elements are included Another indicator would be to check what percentages of major nutrients in the mix are "available." This mean that the elements are in a form useable by the plant. If the percentage of avail ability is not listed on the package, this information also can be gained by

ading the percentage of "water solu-
ility." If you're using a tablet slow
elease form of fertilizer, this is not a
eliable indicator, however. Compari-
on shop, because often you'll find the
ore expensive brand to be a better
uy in terms of actual nutrients
elivered to the plant. Many house-
lanters include a 100 per cent water
oluble fertilizer in their watering can.

revent Pests' Intrusion

The best defense against pests is
revention. Quarantine newly-pur-
hased plants from the old standbys.
espite how carefully you may have in-
pected a plant prior to its purchase,
n infestation may have gone unno-
ced.

Give your plants a quick check every
me you water. Those that don't look
ght (drooping leaves) are possible
andidates for attack and upon closer
ok you will often find a colony of un-
vited guests.

Most common attackers are red
pider mite (tiny red specks under
aves and webbing), white fly (white
andruff-like specks under leaves that
warm out when hit), and cyclamen
ite, invisible to the eye, but stunted
nd deformed leaves, particularly on
frican violets, are indicators of the
est's presence.

All plants infested with cyclamen
ites should be destroyed. Rescue ef-
rts are fruitless. Red spider, aphid
nd other mite infestations can be
ught successfully, if caught early.

The best control for common mites
chemical spray, originally marketed
r use on pet parakeets, etc. Geisler or
lartz Mountain miticides are very ef-
ective, yet safe.

Mealy bugs are extremely common
nd do great damage to plantlife. They
uck juices from stems and leaves,
ventually stunting and/or killing the
lant. They appear as tiny cotton balls
ound at leaf axils. Most effective
ontrol is daubing them with a cotton
wab saturated in alcohol.

Scale also is a common invader that
eeds on plants. True to their name,

they appear as minute fish scales or
transluscent oyster shells on bark and
stems. One cup of Ivory Snow or other
mild soap (no detergents) mixed with a
gallon of water and swabbed onto
infected areas will help remove the
pest. Protect the soil containers from
solution pollution. After the solution
dries, another application, this time
with a scrubbing action, will dislodge
the scales. Following this step, plants
should be rinsed thoroughly in clear
luke-warm water.

In the event this method is unsuc-
cessful, discard the plant, pot and soil.

Most soil insects such as springtails
(tiny insects that scurry around on
plant surfaces) and gnats (grey and
black flying insects) are not harmful.
Creeping and tunneling animals such
as sowbugs, pillbugs and earthworms
also are harmless and in many instances are beneficial to the plants'
well-being. If they offend the plants'
appearance, control is simple. To each
water-feed solution add, at the rate of 1
tablespoon per gallon, clear ammonia.
Repeat this until all signs of unwel-
come visitors have ceased.

Preventative measures can be taken
to ward off invasion of harmful insects.
Sterilized soil is free of insects and
small animals that creep or tunnel. A
"Vapona" Shell pest strip hung among
plants will cut down on airborne inva-
sions resulting from open windows.

Some Grooming Tips

Dispose of sad sack plants. Nothing
looks worse than a diseased, desiccated
plant that barely hangs on even following treatment for its ills.

For well-rounded, balanced plants,
give each sufficient growing space so
that no leaf or part touches the other.
Give your plants a half turn after every
watering. Window sill growers tend to
become one sided when left alone
because most available light is on the
window side.

When leaf margins become dry and
brown-off, trim them and then look to
your watering practices. This is an indication that you are not watering tho-

roughly and/or you are letting the soil
get too dry between waterings.

Leaf drop? First check for pests and
then for overwatering. Weak stems and
clammy leaves are usually signs that
the soil did not dry out enough between
waterings.

Heavy leaf drop and/or yellowing of
large decorator plants can be signs of
poor watering practices. However, if
they have been growing in the same
place for more than three months, look
for the following: jostling by a human;
banging by a vacuum cleaner; exposure to drafts; rapidly fluctuating
temperatures; or someone finding the
soil a convenient place to dispose of a
drink.

Groom your plants. Remove all yellowing and dead leaves. Pick off all
dead and fading flowers. Scratch up
the top soil with a fork if it has become
compacted. Remove dust and dirt ac-
cumulations on the leaves by giving the
plant a gentle luke-warm shower or
misting. For large plants, wipe down
the foliage with dampened paper
towels.

If top soil has been washed away
where watering has occurred, or there
are holes left from the removal of
weeds in unsterilized soil, top dress by
filling in these low spots with a few
spoonfuls of potting soil.

Top dressing also can mean decor-
ating the top layer of soil with a cover
of sheet moss, white marble chips,
pebbles, sand, redwood chips, etc.

Do not summer plants outdoors even
though many experts advise it. There
are too many adjustments and compli-
cations to contend with for any plant
confined to growing in a pot and solely
dependent on a human for its well-
being.

Pinch plants' growing tips occasionally to keep them within bounds
and to force branching.

This practice cannot be attempted,
however, with plants such as palms.
Pruning is necessary for these plants so
that size is controlled. Because plants
need foliage to grow, prune back only a
portion of their branches at once.

Finally, grow only as many plants as
can be conveniently handled. Enjoy
them without having their care become
a tiresome chore.

Indoor Landscaping Ideas

The Entrance

Above: Two glassed panels on either side of the entry door provide enough light for these decorative tropical plants. Overhead, recessed spotlights offer some supplemental illumination. — Courtesy Tile Council of America.

Right: A skylighted atrium features a compatible planting of, from right to left, Ficus exotica, Fatsia japonica, Dieffenbachia picta 'Rudi Roehrs', Beaucarnea recurvata and trailing from a post is Rubus reflexus.

Above: Hanging baskets can brighten bland corners of any room, such as in this living room. From left to right are Nephrolepis bostoniensis, Chlorophytum comosum 'Variegatum' and Philodendron oxycardium. — Courtesy Regal Rugs.

Above left: Plants that lend themselves to moderate diffused light culture are effectively positioned in front of a window decorated with a beaded curtain. The curtain diffuses the strong sunlight that normally would come through the window. At far right, in front of the lighted graphic, is Nephrolepis exaltata bostoniensis compacta (Dwarf Boston Fern). From left to right in the floor planter are Philodendron x 'New Yorker', Dracaena massangeana fragrans, Dieffenbachia amoena, Dracaena marginata, Philodendron panduraeforme, and Dracaena deremensis 'Warneckei'. Above, these in hanging baskets are from left to right, Nephrolepis exaltata 'Verona', Chlorophytum comosum 'Vittatum' and Cissus antarctica. — Courtesy Virginia Frankel, Interior Decorator.

Above: Ficus benjamina 'Exotica', right, along with upright and weeping forms of Dracaena, warm a modern room decor. Also in the background are potted Chrysanthemums. — Courtesy Champion International.

Right: Repetition often is an attractive way to handle plants indoors as well as in outside groupings. In this case, Rhapsis excelsa is utilized with south sea statuary to brighten the corner of this living room and provide a pleasing accent to the warm wood paneling. — Courtesy Champion International.

Recreation & Dining Areas

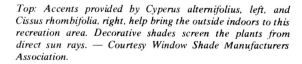

Top: Accents provided by Cyperus alternifolius, left, and Cissus rhombifolia, right, help bring the outside indoors to this recreation area. Decorative shades screen the plants from direct sun rays. — Courtesy Window Shade Manufacturers Association.

Above: Asparagus sprengeri finds use as a shelf-plant in this informal intimate seating area. — Courtesy Tile Council of America.

Above: A variety of ferns are utilized in this dining room. On the floor in the foreground are from left to right, Nephrolepis exaltata 'Whitmanii', Philodendron selloum, and Nephrolepis exaltata. Hanging baskets contain Nephrolepis exaltata 'Verona', and Nephrolepis 'Whitmanii', respectively. On the shelf at right is a small Dracaena marginata. Placed on a table at far right is Chamaedorea elegans. — Courtesy Tile Council of America.

Top: Placed at an east window, this planter contains Nephrolepis exaltata bostoniensis. The planter is lined with watertight sheet metal. Plants rest on a bed of white pebbles. — Courtesy Armstrong Cork Co.

Kitchen & Bath

Above: This kitchen window sill collection of small plants includes Philodendron oxycardium, Dracaena godseffiana, Chlorophytum comosum 'variegatum' and Hedera helix. — Courtesy Firestone Tire & Rubber Co.
Left: In sharp contrast to hard tile surfaces of this bath is a window seat planting of Phoenix roebelenii and Hedera helix 'Denticulata.' The planter is dressed with white stone and the planting is backed by a bamboo curtain that breaks up direct rays of the sun. — Courtesy Tile Council of America.

Starting Plants From Seed

There are so many "best" methods for starting plants from seed, the amount of information published on the subject would fill an encyclopedia. Yet, the simplest, least expensive method will give results equal to the most complicated.

Start by thoroughly washing all containers and tools. Dip them in a 5 per cent clorox solution and rinse in clear water.

The rooting medium should be sterilized and can be a potting soil, vermiculite, sand, Jiffy mix or Jiffy-7.

BEGONIAS

Fill pot with damp soil and make shallow ridges on top by pressing down with a fork. Broadcast the almost microscopic seed as evenly as possible within the indented lines. Slip a plastic bag over two or three supporting plastic straws set in the soil and tuck in under the pot's saucer. This creates a mini-greenhouse that retains the heat and humidity for good germination. There will be no more need to water until the soil dries. Drying actually will take place after the plastic is removed. Because germination is much slower than for other seeds, be patient. It may take two or more weeks before a green leaf appears. Leave the plastic on until the beginnings of two or more leaves appear. Wait several more days, then thin out the plants, using a tweezer to remove the weak. Water mist daily until plantlets harden off and pot up into 2-in. containers. When the plants become rootbound, shift them into 4-in. pots.

COLEUS

A clear plastic refrigerator storage container or any other clear plastic container with or without cover makes an excellent seed starter. A cover can be improvised if none is present by

reading clear plastic across the top.
Spread a one-half inch layer of para-
[ke]t gravel or sand on the container's
[bo]ttom, then a layer of vermiculite so
[th]at this material is within an inch
[fr]om the top. Moisten thoroughly, then
[ut]ilizing the fork method, make inden-
[ta]tions in the medium and spread seed.
[Se]al the container with its cover or
[pl]astic wrap until leaflets appear.
[W]here a rigid plastic cover is used,
[ve]nt the container by slowly raising the
[co]ver as plants grow. Pinch holes in
[im]provised covers. Remove covers
[co]mpletely when two true leaves are
[fo]rmed. Harden off for a few days and
[th]en transplant into individual 2-inch
[gr]owing pots or directly into 4-inch
[po]ts filled with a mix of one part peat-
[m]oss to one part potting soil.

Even though it takes five days or less
[by] this method to germinate the seed
[an]d about three weeks to form true
[le]aves, there is no need to rush the
[po]tting up. Several at a time can be
[d]one. I prefer to wait awhile, water
[fe]eding the plants in the germination
[be]d when the soil medium reads moist
[ha]lf way into the vermiculite layer. In
[th]is manner, especially in the case of
[m]ixed varieties, I can better select the
[fa]nciest, strongest and most colorful
[se]edlings for further growth.

[G]ERANIUMS AND JIFFY-7

Geraniums in three days! Not only
[w]ith geraniums, but with marigolds,
[b]alsam, zinnias and coleus. Tomato
[se]edlings popped up in five days and
[b]egonias in eight. By far the easiest
[an]d quickest, this method is more ex-
[p]ensive, but you get results.

Jiffy-7's come as compact, flat, net
[co]vered dry circles that appear to
[co]nsist mainly of peatmoss. Saturated
[w]ith water they quadruple in height.
[W]hen this occurs, punch a shallow
[h]ole in the center and drop two or three
[se]eds in. For best germination, place
[ea]ch unit in a covered plastic container
[an]d seal as with seeds planted in ver-
[m]iculite. Follow the same procedure,
[b]ut do not shift into 2-inch pots. Grow
[un]til two true leaves form and hair-like
[ro]ots start to grow out through the en-
[cl]osing net. When this occurs, shift
[d]irectly into 4-inch pots.

Although it is not necessary, I prefer
to remove the net because it does not
break down readily. Root development
may be impaired.

WHEN YOU'RE ABSENT...

Most plants, grown in the kinds of
mixes I've recommended, will hold up
without additional water for about five
days if they are moved away from
direct sunlight and given partial shade.

If you plan to be away much longer,
hire the services of a plant sitter, or ask
a friendly neighbor to come in and
water. Although your plants will show
dissatisfaction with a foreign touch,
they will survive until your return.
Boarding them out with a local greenhouse also can be a solution if you plan
an extended vacation. When none of
these is feasible, give your plants to
someone who will love them and start
anew when you return.

WHY MICROCLIMATES?

The purpose of creating a humid
microclimate is to protect moisture-
sensitive plants from the over-dry environment of most households. Two
methods are in wide-spread use today.

First of these is the pebble tray. A
low ceramic dish, planter, ash tray or
sheet metal tray that is waterproof is
filled with pebbles and only enough
water so that the top layer of pebbles
remains nearly dry. Pots of growing
plants are set upon the pebbles.
Moisture-laden air rises to envelope the
plants' foliage.

Acting in the same manner is the
moist bed. A planter is filled with soil,
peatmoss, perlite, sand, pebbles or vermiculite that is kept continually moist.
Saucers of growing plant material are
placed on the moist bed.

Repotting Your Plants

After a plant has been in your possession for one to several months, you'll probably notice that growth has made it top-heavy or that hair-like roots are reaching for additional growing space through the pot's drain holes.

Although some plant varieties thrive under such conditions, heavy foliar and root growth are signs that most plants need repotting.

Small plants grown in pots up to six inches can be easily handled by the novice. Anything larger should be done by a knowledgeable florist or professional indoor gardener. Repotting of large subjects, such as tropical palms, dracaenas and ficus should be done within the home where possible loss from shock, caused by the actual transplant and transportation to and from a shop, is reduced to a minimum.

Following is a step-by-step procedure you can follow when repotting:

A

C

B

D

F

A. The assignment is the repotting of an extremely top-heavy and pot-bound nutmeg scented thyme.

B. Utilize a pot one size larger than the one from which the plant is to be transferred. For example, if a plant is growing in a 3" x 3" pot, procure a 4" x 4". To obtain pot dimensions, measure the inside diameter and outside height from lip to bottom.

C. Prepare the container to accept its new resident by placing a thin layer of pebbles on the bottom of the pot, or bits of clay pot. This provides for good drainage and prevents soil seepage after watering. Fill the balance of the pot with a suitable soil mix and moisten thoroughly by setting in a pan of water while at the same time watering in from the top. This method assures thorough saturation. Form a pocket deep and wide enough so that when the plant is placed into it, the soil level will be at the same point on the plant it was in the original container.

D. Slip the plant from its old container by supporting it with four fingers at soil level; upending the pot and tapping the bottom gently.

E. Set the plant into the pre-formed pocket, tamp in soil from side walls and water thoroughly as instructed in Step C.

F. The newly potted plant should be shaded 1-2 days to minimize stress.

Try Growing Topiaries

Try your hand at growing and **training simple topiaries and standards.**

The easiest to do are the standards such as geraniums, coleus or any other plant that lends itself to growing only on one stem so that it eventually can be developed into a shapely small tree.

This is done by removing all side growth and leaves, yet permitting 4-6 top growth leaves on the main stem. As other leaves form, continue to remove the lowest two, until the plant reaches the desired height. At this point, pinch the growing tip to force branching. **When each branch forms 4-6 leaves,** pinch out their growing tips until a round, bushy head has been formed.

Grow your plants as you would untrained specimens, observing soil medium, sunlight, fertilization and pruning rules.

Other simple topiaries are those trained to a wire form such as the hedera helix "ivy" swan and the sempervivum tectorum calcareum "Hens and chicks" turtle. The ivy is planted directly into the soil of a small, yet heavy decorative asbestos planter that will not topple as the trained plant grows. The turtle, with its sunloving "hens-and-chicks" is first lined with sheet moss to prevent soil spill. Filled with a mix of one part peatmoss to one part soil it is then covered over, with more sheet moss, into which the "hens-and-chicks are inserted. The only watering required is misting when the soil becomes almost bone dry.

Grow Small Tomatoes Inside

Yes, tomatoes can be grown and harvested from a window sill planting. Of course, they won't be the big hearty varieties found in most vegetable gardens, but they will gratify your taste buds with the flavor of fresh-picked fruit.

Small fruited varieties such as W. Atlee Burpee's "Pixie," started indoors from seed on a sunny window and grown to maturity should take about 52 days from germination to harvest. To keep these plants bearing, pick the fruit as it ripens.

Cross-pollination is necessary for good fruit production. Therefore, two plants should be placed in each pot. Because there is no wind to achieve cross-pollination, the plants will need to be shaken gently during flowering or dipping a small artist's brush into each flower, thus carrying the pollen from one to another. In this manner, each flower will be fertilized.

If your plants become top heavy, stake them by plunging a bamboo stick into the center of the pot and using twist ties to fasten main stems and branches.

Waterfeed when the dip stick is damp two-thirds up from the bottom. The potting medium should consist of one part peatmoss and one part potting soil.

Experiment With Pineapples

1. Purchase a ripe pineapple.

Pineapples can be grown as hous plants. The edible tropical Bromeli is available wherever fruit is sold. Sti rich green foliage is the principal a traction to the houseplant hobbyist, y the benefit of obtaining fruit after year of growth is added incentive.

Although rooting and growing su cess can be achieved with ma varieties, I have the best results wi "Sugar Loaf," grown in Hawa Because growers attempt to preve propagation elsewhere, the cent leaves of the rosette are cut out down the core. Therefore, when selecti your fruit, even though some will gro without the center, try to find one th has not been tampered with or showi just partial removal.

Attempt to gauge ripeness of fru without attempting to pull cent leaves. For the plant's cultural requir ments follow recommendations give for Bromeliads.

Step-by-step, here is the way to e tablish this plant in the home enviro ment.

2. *Lop off its head.*

3. *Remove excess fruit and peel off lower leaves to expose potential roots. [Brown roots]*

4. *Prepare a pot filled with a mix of one part peatmoss to one part potting soil. Sand shown in the prepared planting pocket is there to illustrate the pocket's depth.*

5. *Set the new plant into the pocket and tamp soil around it.*

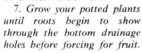

6. *Label and place the plant on a west window sill.*

7. *Grow your potted plants until roots begin to show through the bottom drainage holes before forcing for fruit.*

8. *The plant and a ripe apple should be placed in a plastic bag and sealed. Place this in a semi-shady location. The gas released by the apple stimulates the plant to produce fruit. After two weeks of this treatment, remove the plant from the bag and return it to the west window location.*

9. *After the apple treatment, the central fruit stalk has begun to develop.*

10. *Immature fruit begins to appear.*

WATER ROOTING

A. *Follow steps 1, 2 & 3, and then set head into a glass of water. Waterfeed when you do your other plants, by dripping some water into the top vase.*

B. *When a strong set of roots has developed, pot up the plant as in steps 4-6.*

Gift Plants' Lives Can be Extended

Holiday gift plants, such as azalea, cyclamen, poinsettia, cineraria, Easter lilies, and hydrangeas, are a joy, but difficult to save when blooms fade. Bought in their prime, these greenhouse-forced plants have a difficult time adjusting to the kind of atmosphere encountered in the average indoor environment. At best, you can attempt to wage a holding action until the plants die or manage to survive long enough so they can be placed in the garden after the chance of frost is over.

Since many gift plants are only grown for one burst of beauty, enjoy them, then dispose when blooms fade. Tulips and paper white narcissus, lily-of-the-valley pips, Christmas peppers and Christmas cherries are rarely saved.

To keep gift plants looking attractive as long as possible; unwrap them as soon as they arrive, water thoroughly and place in an east or west window that remains rather cool. An ideal temperature is 65 degrees F. Avoid placement near a heating unit or where drafts are present. When the plants and their blossoms have passed their prime, attempt growing them in the same location until they either expire or the time has arrived for transplanting in the garden.

Azaleas, Easter lilies, hydrangeas, and daffodils often will survive and adapt to the garden. In frost-free areas, poinsettias, cyclamen and clivia sometimes will make the transition.

HIPPEASTRUM

Gorgeous and flamboyant are terms that can best describe these durable, winter-blooming bulb aristocrats. With proper care they can be carried from year to year. In some instances it has been reported that the same bulb has been passed on from one generation to another. Available from October through late December, new bulbs may be purchased potted or unpotted. For best results and enjoyment, buy the largest bulbs available. For the unpotted bulb, find a plastic or clay pot having drainage holes, that is two inches in diameter larger than the broadest part of the bulb. Fill the bottom of the pot with a layer of chard or gravel for good drainage. On top of this, layer with a light covering of horticultural charcoal. Fill the remainder with an all purpose potting soil, leaving enough space to set the bulb so that only two-thirds of its surface is covered with soil. Water thoroughly and place the pot in a warm dark area until the flower stalk and/or foliage is about six inches high. Since this should take about five weeks, be sure the soil does not dry out during this rooting and growing period. Water thoroughly when the dipstick reads damp one third up from the bottom. When plants have developed stalk and leaves, move them to your sunniest window where they soon will produce magnificent, colorful trumpet-like blossoms. After the blooms are spent, remove the flower stalk and permit the foliage to continue growing. This is necessary to build up the bulb and prepare it for next year's bloom. Although some plants will retain their foliage from year to year, most will go dormant with the resulting loss of foliage. This is their resting period. When this occurs, move the plant to a low light environment and water only when soil dries out completely. Continue this treatment until late fall, then repeat the growing cycle. Unless the bulb has outgrown its container, do not repot.

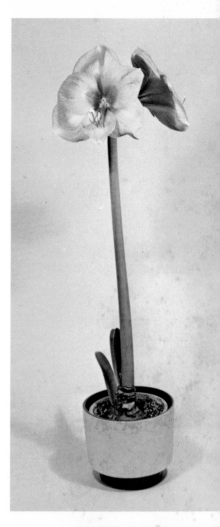

Hippeastrum - Amaryllis

Azalea 'Red Wing'

Poinsettias

Cyclamen

Cineraria

17

The Compatibles

Although unrelated, these are plants that can be grown together. Essentially, they all have the same light, soil, temperature, humidity and water requirements.

Above: With an artificial light unit or greenhouse, varying compatibility can be achieved. Miniature roses, Anthurium scherzerianum and various violets find ideal living conditions in this unit.

Right: This attractive dish garden contains Sansevieria , Philodendron, Dieffenbachia, Peperomia and Dracaena. All do well when placed in an area receiving low to moderate diffused light.

Far Right: Four in a saucer. A small collection to enjoy with minimum care when placed in moderate diffused light. Dominating the arrangement are Peperomia varieties obtusifolia, obtusifolia variegata and caperata. Pilea microphylla rounds out the collection.

Above: Mix 'em and Match 'em is a logical title for this grouping because of 'specimens' similar growth habits. In the back row, left to right, are Codiaeum 'Gloriosum superbum', Podocarpus macrophylla 'Maki' and Dracaena sanderiana. In the front row, left to right, are Dieffenbachia picta 'Rudi Roehrs', Aglaonema simplex and Dieffenbachia picta maculata).

Below: A multi-light level composition can be accomplished in your home similar to this one. In the hanging basket is Sedum morganium, a plant requiring full light. Requiring light in the moderate range are Dracaena fragrans massangeana, the tall plant; and in the right foreground Ligustrum lucidum. Requiring low-medium light is the base planting of Nephrolepis bostoniensis.

Above: A collection of plants that respond well to moderate diffused light can be attractive in a terrarium. Included are Pteris multifida, Asplenium nidus, Syngonium Aglaonema, Hedera helix, Saxifragae, and Pilea panamiga. A chameleon, at right, finds the environment pleasing.

Below: A mini-landscape can be achieved utilizing this grouping of floor plants. The decorative Spaeth planters unify the composition. From left to right are Dracaena deremensis 'Warneckei', Dieffenbachia 'Exotica Perfection', Ficus benjamina 'Exotica' and Brassia actinophylla.

Plants Tolerant of Low Light

There is a large selection of attractive, decorative plants that will adapt and survive in this light even though they prefer to grow and perform in much brighter areas.

Typical low-light situations include north windows and those overlooking shaftways, hallways and entranceways. Interiors, away from windows, that receive artificial light either from recessed ceiling units, downlights, table or floor lamps also are classified as low-light areas.

To obtain best results under these conditions, plants should be exposed to light a minimum of 10 hours a day. Plants grown in low-light situations require little care other than routine maintenance. Growth is severely curtailed and because of this the need for food and other growth elements is not as great.

An occasional move to stronger light for a few days at 2-week intervals or the installation of overhead downlights that are kept on for 24 hours once every week will help decorative accent plants survive an abnormal light environment.

Because dark areas at home or in the office are notorious dust, disease and insect pest collectors, it is vital that good plant hygiene be practiced. Removal of withered and dead foliage plus frequent cleaning of the foliage with a misting device or with dampened paper towels are basic to maintaining plant health.

Aglaonema 'pseudobracteatum'

Aglaonema 'pseudobracteatum'
Aglaonema elegans 'Fransher'
Aglaonema (Schismatoglottis) roebelinii

A convenient test for measuring a low light location is to hold a magazine between the light source and proposed site. Any shadow cast will be extremely faint, and only appear at the upper end of the foot candle range appearing on this page. Where the shadow is most distinct, place plants with highest light requirements.

Aglaonemas are favorites of the houseplanter and interior landscaper because they adapt well to indifferent light; heavy traffic situations and erratic climate. Their varied forms, attractive foliage and slow growing habits (up to three feet) make them a most useful plant for dark, hard-to-grow areas. Proof of their sturdiness is illustrated by the two plants that have been growing on the executive floor of the National Maritime Union Building New York City for over eight years. T only source of light is from overhe ceiling fixtures. Arid heat is blown them in daytime business hours, wh on the weekend, a chill fills the buil ing. Grow these plants in a soil th consists of a one to one mix of potti soil and peatmoss. Water thorough only when the soil is almost bone d and when the dipstick reads one qua ter moist up from the bottom. An occ sional water misting and foliage clea ing with a water dampened cloth w keep the leaves shiny and crisp.

Aglaonema elegans 'Fransher'

Aspidistra elatior
(Cast-Iron Plant)

Aglaonema (Schismatoglottis) roebelinii

Aspidistra elatior
(Cast-Iron Plant)

If you can't grow "Cast-iron plant," I suggest that you give up on indoor gardening. It is the most tolerant of all plants and can withstand a wide range of temperatures, low humidity and almost total darkness. My grandmother grew a specimen for many years in the space under a stairway. This area was drafty and rarely had more than 25 foot candles of light. The plant received a bit more light when it was brought into the basement kitchen once a month for watering and cleaning. For optimum growth Aspidistras prefer an evenly moist soil mix high in peat and loam. A partially shaded area receiving 250-500 foot candles of light, high humidity and a daytime temperature of 65-70 degrees F. with a 10 percent drop at night will produce attractive lush foliage. The ideal soil mix is one part potting soil to one part peatmoss. Water when the dipstick is moist two thirds up from the bottom.

Dieffenbachia amoena
(Giant Dumbcane)

Dieffenbachia 'exotica'

Dieffenbachia amoena
(Giant Dumbcane)

Dieffenbachia 'exotica'

Dieffenbachia picta (maculata)
(Spotted Dumbcane)

Dieffenbachia 'Rudi Roehrs'
(Gold Dieffenbachia)

Average height at maturity, four to five feet and foliage length 6 to 12 inches. Decorative plants that perform well in the warm, dry conditions found in most interiors at home or work. They adapt well to heavy traffic situations, occasional neglect and survive in light as low as 50 foot candles.

Small plants are often used in dish gardens, as table plants, in planters, in dividers or in a floor grouping. Larger individual plants make spectacular accent plants in offices as well as in the home. Growing medium should consist of one part peatmoss to two parts potting soil. Water only when dipstick is moist one third up from bottom. The large leaves should be kept dust free by wiping gently, both top and bottom, with damp paper towels.

Dieffenbachia picta (maculata)
(Spotted Dumbcane)

Dieffenbachia 'Rudi Roehrs'
(Gold Dieffenbachia)

Dracaena marginata (gracilis)
(Madagascar Dragon Tree)

Dracaena sanderiana
(Ribbon Plant)

Dracaena godseffiana
(Gold Dust Dracaena)

This attractive, tolerant tropical foliage plant family offers a wide choice of form, texture, color and growing habits. All are top performers in the average environment and will survive in light as low as 50 foot candles.

The godseffianas, sanderianas and small marginatas all make excellent dish garden plants, are fine for compatible terrariums, fillers for planters and dividers, desk and table plants. Dracaena draco, with its two foot long, green, thick, fleshy, sword-like leaves that arise from a crowding rosette, make robust, decorative floor plants. The Dracaena marginata, a favorite decorator plant, is used widely as floor plant specimens in offices and in the home. Their twisting, undulating, stark bare canes topped with bunches of erect or arching deep green straplike foliage, finely margined in yellow or red, creates an airily artistic mood wherever they are placed. Growing medium of one part peatmoss to one part potting soil is best. Water only when dipstick reads one half moist up from the bottom. All these plants enjoy an occasional warm water misting and having their leaves wiped clean with dampened paper towels.

Dracaena marginata (gracilis)
(Madagascar Dragon Tree)

Dracaena godseffiana
(Gold Dust Dracaena)

Dracaena sanderiana
(Ribbon Plant)

Howea forsteriana
(*Kentia Palm*)

Howea forsteriana
(*Kentia Palm*)

A favorite palm for decorative u
where light is poor. An adaptab
sturdy plant that tolerates neglec
heavy traffic, fluctuations in tempera
ture and light as low as 50 foot candle
Performance is better, however, whe
light reaches 200 foot candles. This
the famous potted palm most used i
hotel dining rooms, lobbies and
weddings since the plant lends itself t
any decor. A suitable soil mix is on
part peatmoss to one part potting soi
Water only when dipstick measure
moist one third up from the bottom.

Pandanus utilis
(*Screw Pine*)

Pandanus veitchii
(*Variegated Screw Pine*)

These shrubby tropicals with swor
sharp and shaped foliage are top pe
formers in heavy traffic situations.
minimum care plant that tolerate
wide variations of temperature, draf
and poor light; they can be used effe
tively as floor plants, in planters and
table plants. Although they may eve
tually grow 60 feet under optimu
conditions, their pace can be slowed t
almost a standstill and yet maintain a
attractive aspect. A good growin
medium contains one part peatmoss t
two parts potting soil. Wate
thoroughly when dip stick is moist on
half way up from bottom.

Monstera deliciosa
(*Split Leaf Philodendron*)

Although these plants appear to be philodendrons, they are not. They have woody stems and for indoor growing they are usually attached to wood bark to support their climbing habit. Long offered by florists because of their proven performance indoors and their decorative qualities, these plants are fine for areas that offer as little as 50 foot candles. Home and office temperatures and fluctuations of same do not appear to affect their growth and appearance. To produce and maintain their typical 3-foot, green glossy foliage, light of 500 foot candles or more is necessary or the new growth will revert back to the immature, smaller, less pinnate form. Provide a soil mix consisting of one part peatmoss to one part potting soil. Water when the dipstick measures moist three fourths up from the bottom.

Monstera deliciosa
(*Split Leaf Philodendron*)

Pandanus veitchii
(*Variegated Screw Pine*)

Pandanus utilis
(*Screw Pine*)

Philodendron X 'Burgundy'
Philodendron hastatum
Philodendron laciniatum
Philodendron oxycardium
(*Heartleaf Philodendron*)
Philodendron panduriforme
(*Fiddle-leaf Philodendron*)
Philodendron selloum
(*Lacy Tree Philodendron*)

Start with a philodendron if you question your growing competence. Many will tolerate almost any kind of situation and care. They'll even grow in water.

There are many other kinds of philodendron other than those listed above, but they are not readily available. However, due to a renewed interest in these decorative, easy-to-grow

Philodendron domesticum (hastatum hort.)

Philodendron laciniatum

Philodendron X 'Burgundy'

Philodendron oxycardium
(Heartleaf Philodendron)

and maintain plants, commercial growers are increasing their propagation of the more uncommon varieties. Many of these can survive light as low as 15 foot candles. Most varieties have a climbing or trailing habit and do well in average temperatures, humidity and diffused or artificial light. They can be easily trained to grow on poles or suspended in hanging baskets. The "self-headers," though compact in growth, will tend to climb as they mature. A suitable soil mix is one part peatmoss to one part potting soil. Water when the dipstick reads moist two thirds up from the bottom.

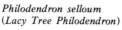

Philodendron panduriforme
(Fiddle-leaf Philodendron)

Philodendron selloum
(Lacy Tree Philodendron)

27

Sansevieria trifasciata laurentii
(*Gold Band Sansevieria*)

Sansevieria trifasciata 'Hahni'
(*Birdsnest Sansevieria*)

Sansevieria trifasciata
(*Snake Plant*)

Sansevieria trifasciata Laurentii
(*Gold Band Sansevieria*)

Sansevieria guineensis
(*Bow-String Hemp*)

Sansevieria trifasciata
(*Snake Plant*)

Sansevieria trifasciata 'Hahnii'
(*Birdsnest Sansevieria*)

Sansevieria trifasciata Laurentii
(*Gold Band Sansevieria*)

Since there aren't many plants grown commercially to choose from that adapt well to low light, I have included the Sansevierias that will tolerate almost anything. They can be grown in bright, medium or low light. Even extended periods of bone dry soil appear to have little effect on their health. The only things that do prove detrimental are overwatering and chilling. Their preference for light is in the medium range at about 500 foot candles. Average temperatures and humidity are preferred, but fluctuations of these really do not have any apparent effect. A suitable potting soil should consist of one part peatmoss to one part potting soil. Water when the dipstick is moist one quarter up from the bottom.

Scindapsus aureus (Mature Form)
(*Devil's Ivy*)

Although they have the same gro habits, performance, uses and cultu requirements, these look alikes are philodendrons. They prefer to grow a soil that is permitted to go nearly before given a thorough watering. soil should be heavier than most ting soils and consist of two parts ting soil to one part peatmoss. these plants also find water a g growing medium. The plant does in average temperatures and light the 100-200 foot candle range. W exposed to greater light little differe in performance is noticed. Water w the dip stick reads moist one-third from the bottom.

Selaginella emmeliana
(*Sweat Plant*)

Closely related to ferns, this p ticular shade-loving, moss-like cree is an excellent subject for low li terrariums where its preference shade, warmth and high humid exists. Brown curling tips indicate t humidity is too low. For best res keep a cover over the terrarium to tain moisture in order to recreate rain forest atmosphere that keeps t beauty happy. It also is an ideal wa greenhouse subject.

Spathyphyllum 'Clevelandii'
(*White Flag*)

Excellent for the novice, these f foliage plants adapt easily to light low as 20 foot candles. They ma beautiful floor plants as well as plan subjects used singly or in masses. F for borders in interior planters, t also make fine background mater that serves as foil for seasonally placed flowering plants. A top p former where there is indirect lig average temperature and humidi they will bloom profusely and give of delicate fragrance in light of 50 more foot candles. An optimum s mix consists of one part peatmoss one part potting soil. Watering sho occur when the dipstick is moist t thirds from the bottom.

Scindapsus aureus (*Mature Form*)
(*Devil's Ivy*)

Tolmiea menziesii
(*Piggy Back Plant*)

Tolmiea menziesii
(*Piggy Back Plant*)

A favorite of interior decorators for home use when an inexpensive, small, lush plant is required to soften and/or accent a particular space such as the floor, table, unlighted entrance way or even in a hanging basket. Although delicate in appearance, this versatile hardy native of Alaska, that grows along the coastal region as far south as California, tolerates and adapts well to a wide range of light and growing conditions. This plant is winter hardy outdoors and often will retain its green foliage when grown in sheltered spots. The plant is a frequent topic of conversation by those who first see it because of plantlets growing from mature leaves' bases. Tolmiea will survive in low light of about 50 foot candles, but does best in diffused light of about 500 foot candles. The plant prefers a damp heavy soil that is permitted to go nearly dry before each watering. To prepare a good soil mix utilize one part potting soil to one part of peatmoss. Water either when leaves begin to wilt or the dipstick is moist one third up from the bottom.

Selaginella emmeliana
(*Sweat Plant*)

Spathyphyllum 'Clevelandii'
(*White Flag*)

Plants of Moderate Light Culture

Adiantum tenerum 'Wrightii'

A simple method for testing whether there is enough light available for plants requiring moderate amounts of light is to hold up a magazine between the light source and proposed plant location. The shadow cast will be distinct. Where the shadow is most pronounced, place plants requiring light at the upper end of the foot candle range appearing on this page.

This is the intensity of light that certain plants will adapt to and perform satisfactorily if available for at least eight hours a day. Although the plants may be exposed to direct sun rays in this situation for a period of 2-3 hours, the primary light source is diffused light.

Moderate diffused light can usually be found in or near an east or south window where there is a deep overhang, overgrown trees or shrubs screening the windows. It also may occur where screens are left on year round, where there is outside grillwork, or an adjacent building casts a heavy shadow.

If you don't have a light meter, place your hand into the area where you plan to establish house plants. If your hand casts a shadow, it is an indication of 100 or more footcandles of light present.

Often, shades, blinds or drapes are utilized to cut down on entry of light into a house, especially where it can be destructive to interior furnishings or offensive to people living in these rooms. Light diffused by these barriers still will be sufficient to grow plants in the 100-1000 foot candle range.

Ash soot and grime coating outside of windows in metro areas also can diffuse light and thus provide suitable growing conditions for plants liking moderate illumination.

Adiantum tenerum 'Wrightii'

The plant is well worth your patience and growing space while it adapts to your home environment. Though it will survive in average room temperatures, it does require high humidity for best results. Humidity can be increased by daily water misting or placing the pot on a moist gravel bed. Another trick is to grow the plant in a compatible grouping, thus forming a humid microclimate.

A forest floor plant, the maidenhairs prefer a moist growing medium, filtered strong light and a minimum of disturbance. This compact, slow grower is most appreciated for its delicate emerald-green fan-shaped fronds that grow on sturdy, black wiry stems. It is ideally grown on a shelf, table or even a window sill that does not offer direct sunlight.

Aeschynanthus (Gesneriaceae)
(*Lipstick Vine*)

A favorite, sturdy plant that is suitable for hanging baskets in addition to being a good trailing pot plant. It is happiest grown on an east or west window where the light is filtered. Yet, exposure to direct sunlight for a few hours, during winter months at times when light is weakest, helps maintain leaf quality. Although the plant is tolerant of the average indoor environment, it does prefer a warm, humid location. For best results, an occasional water misting and a cleansing thorough spray under warm water will be most effective for preserving good health. The soil should be high in peatmoss and humus

Aeschynanthus (Gesneriace
(Lipstick Vine)

because of the plant's preference for constantly moist growing medium. best, however, to let the soil dry to o half the level on the dipstick befo thoroughly watering. Healthy, matu plants often bloom in early sprin exhibiting flowers of red accented wi creamy-yellow throats.

Aloe

These highly decorative succulents make excellent subjects for dish gardens or can be attractive specimen plants. They are easily identified by their basal rosettes formed of stiff, succulent spiny leaves. The moisture storing capacity of their thick juicy tender leaves, necessary for survival in their naturally arid habitat, serves them well in household interiors. Utilized in cosmetic formulation and for medicinal purposes, the aloes also find widespread use as just houseplants. Optimum growth is achieved when the plants are placed in areas where light is no more than 500 foot candles. Strong light will cause a browning-off appearance to foliage. Although these plants can withstand arid conditions, they do best in a damp soil environment. A soil mix of peat and vermiculite and loam in equal parts will keep the soil moist. Water thoroughly when the dip stick is moist one third up from the bottom.

Aloe vera chinensis
(Indian Medicine Aloe)

Aloe arborescens
(Octopus Plant)

Aloe africana
(Spiny Aloe)

Aloe ferox
(Ferocious Aloe)

Anthurium scherzerianum
(Flame Plant)

Anthurium scherzerianum
(Flame Plant)

I have not found these beauties difficult to grow in the house on a window sill despite most published information to the contrary. High temperature and humidity lovers such as Anthurium scherzerianum have adapted and bloomed for me on a west window that receives sun about three hours a day during the winter. True, the deep overhang above this window does offer considerable shade, but light measured there often reads well above 1000 foot candles. During the summer months I grow it about two feet away from the glass more to prevent it from rapid drying out than to protect it from the sun. To play it safe, until you acclimate the plant, grow it an no more than 500 foot candles of diffused light. Anthuriums prefer a constantly moist fibrous growing medium such as peat moss or a combination of osmunda and sphagnum. Water when dipstick is moist three quarters up from the bottom.

Aphelandra squarrosa
(*Zebra Plant*)

Aphelandra squarrosa
(*Zebra Plant*)

The attractive, rich green Zebra-striped foliage of this tropical evergreen provides a sparkling accent wherever it is grown. Heavy traffic, typical of offices and public spaces, or even occasional drafts do not appear to affect its well-being. Grown principally for its striking foliage and compact habit, Aphelandras make excellent planter subjects, floor plants and desk plants. Although most commercial size plants average about eight inches high they will in time attain a height up to three feet. They perform well in average temperatures and humidity, but are moisture sensitive. They must be watched for wilting because the soil must be permitted to go almost completely dry between waterings. Soil mix should consist of one part potting soil to one part peatmoss. Water when dipstick reads moist one third up from bottom.

Aucuba japonica variegata
(*Gold Dust Plant*)
Asparagus densiflorus 'Meyers'
(*Plume Asparagus*)

Asparagus densiflorus 'Sprengeri'
(Sprengeri Fern)

paragus densiflorus 'Sprengeri'
rengeri Fern)

paragus densiflorus 'Meyers'
ume Asparagus)

Ideal for hanging baskets, floor and nters, the airy grace of these sturdy, tant relatives of our garden aspara-s are fast becoming favorites of the corator and house planter. They are n in window groupings that form a eze of chartreuse to deep green ereby their needle-like branchlets true leaves) serve to create a natural ep through curtain. Resistant to rage heat and humidity, these na-es of South Africa do appreciate an casional water misting to keep the edles bright and clean. The soil uld never be permitted to dry out npletely if heavy needle fall is to be ided. Too little or too much light cause yellowing of the foliage. ough these plants are not delicate, y will have to be given time to estab-themselves. Don't be upset at first some yellowing and needle fall. Soil uld be kept on the damp side and uld consist of one part peatmoss to parts African violet type potting . For pot plants, water thoroughly en dip stick is moist one third from tom. If you are growing your plants moss-lined hanging baskets, I gest that they be soaked thoroughly a pan of warm water when they are f the weight of a thoroughly

Asplenium (Filices) nidus
(Birdsnest Fern)

saturated plant and its growing medium. Of course, set the plant to drain before returning it to its normal growing situation.

Asplenium (Filices) nidus
(Birdsnest Fern)

Known to tolerate light as poor as 25 foot candles, I prefer to grow the "Birdsnest" at a minimum of 100 foot candles. A fine accent plant for floor, table, grown singly or massed in a planter; the texture and form of its sleek, shiny chartreuse fronds growing up out of a black scaled rosette creates an eyecatching picture wherever this plant is grown. Though at first it may appear delicate, this is not the case. In fact, the leathery fronds supported by a black mid-rib often attain a height of three feet. An easy plant to enjoy and grow, it prefers an evenly damp soil and a 60 — 70 degree F. temperature range. Of course, it will tolerate other than optimum conditions. Grow in an average soil mix containing at least one part peat and one part pot-

ting soil. Water thoroughly when dip-stick reads moist half way up from bottom. Avoid water accumulation in the heart of the rosette so crown rot is averted.

Aucuba japonica variegata
(Gold Dust Plant)

Fine for dish gardens, edging in planters or grown as individual pot plants. Larger specimens available three feet or taller make excellent decorator subjects for heavy traffic areas at home or at work. This hardy, bushy plant has become an indoor favorite because it adapts quickly, tolerates most any environment as well as indifferent care. Though prone to red spider, this pest can be easily controlled with the safe spray used for mite control on pet birds. A natural, non-chemical method is to give the complete plant a brisk, yet gentle shower that reaches all its parts. Soil should consist of two parts potting soil and one part peat moss. Permit the soil to dry out down to a one third moist dip-stick before each thorough watering.

Begonia coccinea
(*Angel Wing Begonia*)

Begonia 'Medora'
(*Troutleaf Begonia*)

Their common name is derived from their paired winglike leaves that are borne on cane-like stems. Free flowering, these fibrous-rooted top performers make attractive, year-round specimens even when not in bloom because of their glossy green spotted silver foliage with undersides of irridescent maroon red. The exquisite small leaved 'Medora' with its trailing habit makes a fine hanging basket subject for window or plant stand. The vigorous, erect habit of coccinea appreciates an occasional pruning to keep it compact and control its tendency to legginess. Permitted to grow at will, Begonia coccinea can attain a height of 15 feet. Definitely a home grower, these plants prefer a humid, airy atmosphere. An occasional bit of sun sneaking through the dense foliage of a tree or shrub will have no ill effects. In fact, this kind of light boost may improve the color intensity of their foliage. Growing medium should consist of one part potting soil to one part peatmoss. This kind of mix permits good soil aeration for these fibrous rooted plants that are prone to root rot if the soil isn't open. Water thoroughly only when the dipstick is moist one half way up from the bottom.

Begonia X 'Cleopatra'
(*Maple Leaf Begonia*)

The Nile green chocolate patterned translucent miniature foliage of this rhizomatous begonia provides you with another one of those robust, decorative leaf plants that add interest to any house plant collection. Excellent as a pot plant, its creeping habit and compact form also make it a fine subject for hanging baskets or trailing shelf plant that requires little growing space. Cultural and environmental requirements are the same as those for Begonia masoniance and the angel wings. Though not illustrated, there are a number of available, good, reliable varieties to grow with similar habits. They include Begonia 'Paul Bryant,' Begonia x 'Joe Hayden,' and Begonia x 'Beatrice Haddrell.'

Begonia Rex masoniana
(*Iron Cross Begonia*)

Begonia X 'Cleopatra'
(*Maple Leaf Begonia*)

Begonia coccinea
(Angel Wing Begonia)

Begonia 'Frosty Dwarf'

Begonia Rex 'Mikado'

Begonia 'Medora'
(Troutleaf Begonia)

Begonia Rex 'Helen Teupel'

Begonia Rex masoniana
(Iron Cross Begonia)

Grown chiefly for its attractive, bristly red-haired, puckered Nile green foliage marked with its distinctive chocolate brown pattern, this plant is an eyestopper whereever it is exhibited. A perfect house plant for the low table or plant stand that does not receive direct light which it finds difficult to adapt to. Grown outdoors in the subtropics such as Florida (Fairchild Gardens in Miami), it is ideally used as a shady border plant where its striking colors and creeping habit are set off to their best advantage. Leaves often grow as large as six inches in diameter. These plants must be protected from direct sunlight and do best at an average temperature of 70 degrees F. both day and night with an atmosphere that is high in humidity. Damp soil of one part potting soil to one part peatmoss is best for required aeration. Water thoroughly when dipstick is moist one half way up from bottom.

Bertolonia 'Mosaica'
(Jewel Plant)

Bertolonia 'Mosaica'

(Jewel Plant)

This gem is a bit tricky because of its high humidity requirement, but it can be grown successfully for your enjoyment in a terrarium. Free flowering with a creeping, low habit, they perform well as long as the humidity is high and the atmosphere is warm. Growing medium should consist of two parts peatmoss to one part African violet potting soil. After adjusting water content in the terrarium, keep it covered most of each day and away from light over 500 foot candles. They do best in the 100-300 foot candle range. Though not widely distributed I do think this plant should be made accessible to the house planter.

Brassaia actinophylla
(Schefflera actinophylla)

Brassaia actinophylla

(Schefflera actinophylla)

This majestic tropical is a plant for almost every interior. In fact, it thrives in the warm, dry atmosphere commonly found in our homes and at work. Although it prefers a sunny environment, it can survive in light as low as 50 foot candles, although this is not recommended for long. Growing medium should consist of one pa peatmoss to one part potting soil. Th soil should be permitted to dry out a most completely between waterings when the dip stick measures moi about one quarter up from the bottom It does appreciate an occasional mis ing or wiping down of the foliage wit damp paper towels to remove accumu lations of dust and grit that are ever where in our atmosphere.

Cereus peruvianus
(Column Cactus)

Cereus peruvianus
(Column Cactus)

This robust, tolerant cactus is available in sizes from six inches to six feet or more. Even though it does prefer a warm, sunny environment, this plant has been known to adapt well to light as low as 50 foot candles. A fine decorator plant for home or office, it appears best as a single large specimen because of its columnar form. The blue-green color, typical of this variety blends well into any decor. It also makes a fine window subject since it will tolerate the wide variations of temperature encountered near the glass. Grow it dry in poor light. That is: only water in spring and summer one week after the soil has gone bone dry. In winter and fall wait at least two weeks after the soil becomes bone dry. Give it a dilute fish emulsion water feed only when you see signs of new growth. Soil mix: all purpose mix for cactus.

Aechmea chantinii
(Amazonian Zebra Plant)

Aechmea mariae reginae
(Queen Aechmea)

Vriesea splendens 'major'
(Flaming Sword)

Bromeliaceae
Aechmea chantininii
(Amazonian Zebra Plant)
Aechmea mariae reginae
Queen Aechmea)
Vriesia splendens 'major'
Flaming Sword)

Most members of this genus are epiphytes, clinging to trees and sustaining themselves with the water and detritus that fall into their cups. The varieties illustrated are easily available and usually grown as decorative pot plants. They adapt well to most indoor environments and tolerate fluctuations in temperature and heavy traffic. Each will survive in light of 100 foot candles, but prefers 500. These plants will keep their mature form and attractive appearance for nearly a year. Blossoms, which hold for nearly two months, dry out, but maintain their color for at least another three months. Since the mature plant only blooms once, new plants must be started from offshoots found at the base or from the crown. A suitable medium is all sphagnum moss or one part potting soil to one part peatmoss. Soak the soil thoroughly once a week and waterfeed through the vase whenever it appears dry.

Chamaedorea elegans
(*Dwarf Mountain Palm*)
Chamaedorea elegans 'Bella'
(*Neanthe Bella*)

All are decorator favorites for heavy traffic areas with average humidity and temperature. Both Chamaedorea elegans and elegans 'bella' are used frequently as floor plants, in borders or as small potted plants for a low table where light is poor. Chamaedorea erumpens, with bamboo canes, make fine, large tree form plants where a dark corner needs livening up.

Chamaedorea elegans
(*Dwarf Mountain Palm*)

Chamaedorea elegans 'Bella'
(Neanthe Bella)

All these small, thin-leaved palms prefer the shade and will tolerate light as low as 40 foot candles. Exposure to sunlight will bleach their leaves. Growing medium should consist of one part peatmoss to one part potting soil. Water thoroughly when dipstick is moist one half up from the bottom.

Cibotium schiedei
(Mexican Tree Fern)

In spite of its delicate appearance, Cibotium schiedei, the "Mexican tree-fern" is one of the most durable ferns available today. It adapts well to the average environment and is frequently used on the floor or as a plant stand object. The airy grace of the three to five foot apple green fronds that grow out from an attractive fibrous trunk are a welcome addition to a room of any period. Although they are usually offered for sale when they are about four feet tall in their pots, they eventually, over the years, can attain a height of 15 feet. Growing medium of one part peatmoss to two parts potting soil should be permitted to go almost dry before each watering. The dipstick moisture measure of one third from the bottom is safest.

Chamaerops humilis
(European fan palm)

The slow-growing, bushy habit of this full-green palm is often used to good advantage as a decorative single speci-men floor plant that does not outgrow its assigned space. It rarely grows beyond three feet and adapts to average temperature and humidity. Although it prefers higher light inten-sity, it will survive in 75 foot candles. A damp growing medium of one part peatmoss to one part potting soil serves as excellent support.

Cibotium schiedei
(Mexican Tree Fern)

Chamaerops humilis
(European fan palm)

Cissus antarctica
(Kangaroo Vine)

Cissus rhombifolia
(Grape Ivy)

Cissus rhombifolia 'Mandaiana'
(Bold Grape Ivy)

Cissus

Grape-like vines that climb by tendrils. These plants tolerate average temperatures, light and humidity. For best growth they do prefer some direct sun one to three hours a day, but do adapt well to diffused light of low intensity. Soil should consist of one part peatmoss to two parts potting soil. Water thoroughly only when dipstick is moist one third up from bottom. An occasional water misting does wonders to perk up and cleanse the leaves.

Cissus antarctica
(Kangaroo Vine)

This superior hanging basket plant with its bright, shiny, leathery leaves that grow up to six inches in length will surprise you if you stand close to it for any length of time. Heat and light sensitive, the plant's tendrils will brush you ever so gently in their attempt to gain a foothold onto anything near it.

Foliage is quilted, silvery in color with center variegation of violet to red-purple. Sunken leaf veins are moss green. Backs of the leaves are irridescent maroon. It makes a fine trailing pot plant or trellis subject.

Cissus rhombifolia
(Grape Ivy)

At first glance the thick, leathery dark green three to four inch leaves of these are so grape-like in appearance that you have to look twice at these hanging basket plants before you realize they are natural copy-cats. They exhibit long grape-like tendrils and the wood is typical of the wine vine.

Cissus rhombifolia 'Mandaiana'
(Bold Grape Ivy)

A sport of rhombifolia, this plant has a compact, bushy habit instead of the looser, more widely spaced groupings of its leaves of three. Foliage is smaller, thicker and darker green than the parent. A top rated performer.

Clusia rosea

A sturdy, tolerant tropical evergreen tree that is favored by decorators and house planters who seek the kind of character it affords. Average heights available in the pot range from three to five feet even though this plant growing

in the wild can attain a height of feet. It has horizontal branches and t fat, obovate, thick, leathery de green, opposite eight inch leaves ha no lateral veins. Although this pla can survive in light as low as 50 fe candles, my experience has been th there is little or no change in leaf co and texture. However, left in this e vironment for an extended perio there is considerable leaf loss. For l light culture, a cool, dry atmosphere best. Growing medium should cons of one part peat to one part potti soil. Water thoroughly only when di stick is moist one third up fro bottom.

Coccothrinax argentata
(Silver Palm)

This decorative palm usua available in the four to six foot ran and grows as broad as it grows tall wi leaves that divide almost to the base a fan that arches out gracefully. T rich green of each leaf is accented by silvery underside. In the normal cond tions of its native habitat the Coco thrinax argentata may grow as high 40 feet. Tolerant of average temper tures and humidity, it does apprecia an occasional lukewarm shower an move to an area with some sunlight f a few days each month. Grow it in o part peatmoss to one part potting so Water only when dipstick is moist o third up from the bottom.

Columnea
(Candy Corn)
Columnea x (Vega)
(Goldfish Bush)

Crimson bilabiate Columneas a trailing epiphytic gesneriads th adapt well in the home when grown pot plants, trailing plants for shelf cu ture and in hanging baskets for wi dow display and enjoyment. Mo varieties bloom in the spring providin the plants have been been pinche back. As with many plants of all kind they must be permitted to break apic growth for bud inception. The leave grow in pairs that are often unequal size and different in shape. The blade may be ovate to pinnate in form an can be as small as one inch, as long a three inches and as wide as two an one-half inches. These dimension

Columnea x (Vega)
(Goldfish Bush)

Coccothrinax argentata
(Silver Palm)

Clusia rosea

Columnea
(Candy Corn)

differ with each variety. The semi-woody stems root easily at the nodes (axils where the leaves come forth). Depending on variety, the two lipped tubular flowers are colored scarlet, crimson, yellow, pink or orange. These can vary in length from one-half inch to four inches. Tolerant of average temperatures and humidity, they do prefer an air moisture content of at least fifty per cent. Water misting does help a bit. The growing medium of one part peatmoss to one part potting soil should be watered thoroughly when the dipstick reads one half moist up from the bottom.

Crassula argentea
(Jade Plant)

Crassula argentea

(Jade Plant)

These sturdy, adaptable succulents make ideal subjects for interiors at work or in the home. They tolerate average environmental conditions, are not overly sensitive to drafts, neglect or low temperatures and can survive in poor light. They perform best when pot bound, so don't be in a rush to repot them. Crassula argentea is available in sizes from three inches to three feet. They can be used as desk plants, in compatible dish gardens and terrariums or as a window sill pot plant. Mature, large specimens make fine floor plants up near a window or in a hallway that receives strong light but no direct sunlight. These plants tend to sunburn if exposed too long in direct

sun. Crassula argentea is a succulent shrub that can grow 10 feet in height and equally wide. It has a thick fleshy trunk, and undulating, thick, fleshy branches that form freely. The leaves are glossy dark green, thick succulent one to two-inch pads that are flat on the undersides and convex on top. Mature plants will produce masses of starry-white flowers from December to March.

Other commercially availabl varieties with similar habits an tolerant characteristics:

Crassula argentea variegata

(Variegated Jade Plant)

Leaves have a rounded apex and ar colored green-grey and variegated wit cream to almost orange.

The foliage is a bit narrower an more pointed than the others di cussed. Its green, glossy leaves hav sharply contrasted striped variegatio of grey and white, with dark pink clos to the margins. Growing medium fo Crassulas should consist of one par peatmoss to two parts potting soil fo cactus. Water thoroughly when th dipstick is moist only one quarter u from the bottom.

Crossandra infundibuliformis
(Firecracker Flower)

Crossandra infundibuliformis

(Firecracker Flower)

An excellent pot plant for the warm strongly lighted window within 500 t 1000 foot candles that does not receiv direct sunlight. A compact, leafy shrubby habit plant, its three to five inch long thin glossy green, ovat leaves are attractive the year-round This plant blooms freely from earl spring to mid-October. Clustered tubular, salmon flowers appear out of bracted spike that grows from the lea axil. They perform best in a warm humid atmosphere, yet adapt well t the home environment. Water sensi tive, their fibrous roots should not b permitted to dry out and burn. T

Ctenanthe oppenheimiana tricolor
(Never-Never Plant)

Davallia trichomonoides canariensis
(Carrot Fern)

Cyperus alternifolius
(Umbrella Plant)

avoid the possibility of root rot remove all standing water an hour after watering. A good growing medium is one part peatmoss to one part potting soil. Water thoroughly when dipstick is moist one half way up from bottom.

Ctenanthe oppenheimiana tricolor
(Never-Never Plant)

Ideal as a striking individual pot plant or planter filler, this gay, colorful narrow leaved plant offers great contrast and airy height where all green foliage predominates. The tops of these thin, long leaves are splashed with white, olive and jade green, and pink that blushes through from the wine-red back. Adaptable to most interior conditions, it does prefer a warm, moist atmosphere. A good growing medium should consist of one part peatmoss to one part potting soil. Water thoroughly when dipstick is moist one half way up from the bottom.

Cyperus alternifolius
(Umbrella Plant)

These semi-aquatic plants make excellent displays around recirculating fountains and aquariums where these moisture lovers can enjoy the mist rising from the water sources. These plants adapt well to average temperatures and humidity, providing they have a constant source of moisture circulating around them. Their delicate form and graceful growing habit give distinction to any interior. Small potted plants should be set on pebbles in water-filled trays or into decorative ceramic containers with pebbles and water on the bottom. Large, decorative specimens do best when the growing pot is either set atop a pebble tray or into a decorative container with bricks at the bottom. Water level should reach to the top of these bricks. Typical of bog plants, the growing medium can be quite heavy and compacted. I use one-quarter peat moss to three-quarters potting soil. Water only when dipstick is moist one half way up from the bottom.

Davallia solida
(Rabbit's Foot Fern)

Davallia solida
(Rabbit's Foot Fern)
Davallia trichomonoides canariensis
(Carrot Fern)

Davallias derive their common name, "Rabbit's-foot fern" from their typical furry, creeping rhizomes that look so much like a rabbit's foot. Fine hanging basket subjects, they are not the easiest of plants to grow since they do require a high humidity. Once they adapt, however, their decorative and conversation piece qualities are well worth waiting for. For hanging basket culture they prefer to grow in peatmoss, sphagnum or a combination of both. Water by soaking the basket up to its rim in a tub of luke warm water when the planter is half the weight it was when formerly saturated. They are humidity lovers. You can provide additional atmospheric moisture with frequent mistings. Davallias can be grown successfully as pot plants in a growing medium of two parts peatmoss to one part potting soil that is kept evenly damp at all times. This can be accomplished by setting the growing pot into a ceramic dish so that it sits on a layer of pebbles just above the water line. Avoid exposure to direct sunlight.

Dracaena deremensis 'Warneckei'
(Striped Dracaena)

Dracaena deremensis 'Warneckei'
(*Striped Dracaena*)
Dracaena deremensis 'Janet Craig'
Dracaena fragrans massangeana
(*Cornstalk Plant*)
Pleomele reflexa
(*Maylasian Dracaena*)
Pleomele thaloides
(*Lance Dracaena*)

These plants range in height from one to 60 feet. Suitable as decorative background plants or single specimens in tree and shrub forms, they are ideal for light areas where candlepower ranges from 100-200 FC. Optimum growing conditions, however, are: light in the 400-500 foot candle range; a draft-free humid atmosphere; and an average indoor living temperature. These plants prefer to have their roots confined and do best in smaller pots than appear suitable for their size. A suitable soil mix includes one part peatmoss to one part of potting soil. Water only when the dipstick is moist one half way up from the bottom.

Pleomele thaloides
(Lance Dracaena)

Dracaena deremensis 'Janet Craig'

Pleomele reflexa
(Maylasian Dracaena)

Dracaena fragrans massangeana
(Cornstalk Plant)

Dudleya virens (Echeveria insularis)

This plant, adaptable today as it was when it first appeared on earth, is actually a fossil. A survivor from pre-history, it is a forerunner of our present evergreens such as pines. It makes an excellent floor plant for most interiors because of its adaptability and will tolerate fluctuating temperatures and humidity. Grow in a soil of one part peatmoss to one part potting soil. Water when dipstick reads moist one third up from the bottom.

Episcia cupreata 'metallica'
(Kitty Episcia)

Episcia dianthiflora
(Lace Flower Vine)

In the spring and summer this plant is covered with tiny, white, single carnation-like flowers. The creeping, trailing, drooping habits of the Episcias make them fine house plant subjects for hanging baskets, shelf pot-plants, as ground cover in planters or in a compatible terrarium. They are strictly a plant for a house planter who is willing to provide a higher humidity than normal (45-75%) to get the best performance from these exquisite gems. This can be done by setting their pots on pebbles in trays that contain water just below the top layer of pebbles or double potting using the same pebbles and water approach at the bottom of the outer container. Soil mix should consist of one part peatmoss to two parts potting soil for African violets. Water when dipstick is moist two thirds up from bottom. Frequent misting helps.

Euphorbia flanaganii
(Green Crown)

Euphorbia lactea
(Candelabra Cactus)

Euphorbia lactea cristata
(Elkhorn Cactus)

Euphorbia tirucalli
(Pencil Cactus)

Euphorbia ingens
(Candelabra Tree)

Tough ornamentals for the kind of atmosphere we encounter in most interiors. A minimum of care, variations in light and temperature hardly affect them. Although they prefer a warm, dry, bright growing situation, they will adapt to other than perfect conditions and make fine moderate, diffused light subjects. Euphorbia flanaganii makes a fine basket or shelf plant as does

Encephalartos latifrons
(Spiny Kaffir Bread)

Episcia cupreata 'metallica'
(Kitty Episcia)

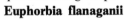

Episcia dianthiflora
(Lace Flower Vine)

Dudleya virens (Echeveria insularis)

An excellent succulent for cool, humid situations, it will tolerate and survive in other than optimum conditions. It makes a fine sill plant where it eventually may grow to a diameter of 10 inches. In an all foliage setting such as a dish garden or planter, it can serve as an outstanding accent with its rosette of thick, waxy, blue-grey leaves tipped with red. Occasional exposure to dappled sunlight is fine. Full sun will give it a sunburn. A good growing medium of one part peatmoss to two parts potting soil for cactus is fine. Water only when dipstick measures moist one third up from the bottom.

Encephalartos latifrons
(Spiny Kaffir Bread)

tirucalli which is frequently grown in tree form attaining a height of six feet or more when staked. Growing medium should consist of one part peatmoss to two parts potting soil for cactus. Water only when bone dry. This means one week after you decide that the soil is completely dry down to the bottom of the pot. Repotting should be done only when the plant cannot be supported in the growing pot by a stake or by itself. These plants do best when their roots are tightly confined. For specimens averaging two feet or taller it is best not to remove them from their growing pot, but to double pot them by setting the pot inside a pot no more than two sizes larger and filling in the area, the bottom and between the walls, with soil so that soil level of the original remains the same.

Euphorbia tirucalli
(Pencil Cactus)

Euphorbia flanaganii
(Green Crown)

Euphorbia lactea
(Candelabra Cactus)

Euphorbia ingens
(Candelabra Tree)

Euphorbia lactea cristata
(Elkhorn Cactus)

Fatsia japonica
(*Japanese Aralia*)

A decorative plant that tolerates fluctuating temperatures and will survive in light as low as 50 foot candles. When planted three to a tub or pan, they make excellent, low, bushy, floor plants. Singly, they are fine for tables, shelves, pebble tray groupings, dish gardens, or in planters where the light can be strong but not in direct sun. Though they prefer cool temperatures from 55 to 60 degrees F., they adapt to warmer situations if there is good air circulation. Soil should consist of one part peatmoss to one part potting soil. Water when dip stick reads two-thirds moist up from the bottom.

Fatsia japonica
(*Japanese Aralia*)

Fittonia verschaffeltii

Fittonia verschaffeltii argyroneura
(*Nerve Plant*)

Fittonia verschaffeltii
Fittonia verschaffeltii argyroneura
(*Nerve Plant*)

A fine, small, decorative plant for the home. Though it tolerates the average environment, it does prefer a higher humidity. Low, creeping to semi-erect in habit, they make excellent basket, shelf and table plants. Also fine for terrariums where they thrive in the warm humid atmosphere. The netted white or pink-red three inch oval leaves are typical of these beautiful gems. Growing medium should consist of one part peatmoss to one part potting soil. Water thoroughly when dipstick reads one third down from the top soil line. To increase humidity set pots on pebbles that are in trays that contain water about three quarters full.

48

Hedera helix 'denticulata'

Helxine soleirolii
(Baby's Tears)

Hedera helix 'Glacier'

Hedera helix 'denticulata'
Hedera helix 'Glacier'

Hedera helix comes in many varieties, forms, sizes, and variations. Some have three lobes, others five that are needle-like, and others have pleated foliage or almost solidly ovate. Natural climbers and trailers, they make fine basket, shelf, trellis and window sill subjects. Any setting is enhanced with their airy grace. Many are hardy outdoor plants that adapt well to the home environment. They do best when grown at a temperature of 70 degrees F. or less. Soil should consist of one part peatmoss to one part potting soil. Water only when dipstick reads moist one half way up from the bottom. They enjoy an occasional warm water misting or luke warm shower.

Helxine soleirolii
(Baby's Tears)

A ground hugging moss-like creeper, this herb exhibits rounded, almost succulent tiny leaves about one-quarter inch in diameter. Growing out from thread-thin branches, the foliage forms dense masses as the leaves spill over each other as they form. Often used on greenhouse floors as ground cover, these decorative miniatures are offered as basket plants and small pot plants. Adaptable to the home atmosphere, they will perform best in a high humidity situation such as a terrarium or set on top of pebbles in a tray partly filled with water. The soil should not get too dry between waterings or else the plant will curl inwards to retain moisture. Many leaves will dry up, resulting in a considerable loss of foliage. Soil should consist of one part peatmoss to one part potting soil. Water thoroughly when dipstick is moist two thirds up from the bottom. If in doubt when to water, look for curling leaves.

Ficus benjamina
(Weeping Fig)

Ficus elastica 'Doescheri'
(Variegated Rubber Plant)

Ficus lyrata (Pandurata)
(Fiddleleaf Fig)

Ficus diversifolia (Lutescens)
(Mistletoe Fig)

Focus radicans 'variegata'
(Variegated Rooting Fig)

Ficus benjamina 'Exotica'

50

Ficus retusa nitida
(*Indian Laurel*)

Ficus stricta 'Philippinense'

Ficus benjamina
(*Weeping Fig*)
Ficus diversifolia (Lutescens)
(*Mistletoe Fig*)
Ficus elastica 'Doescheri'
(*Variegated Rubber Plant*)
Ficus lyrata (Pandurata)
(*Fiddleleaf Fig*)
Ficus retusa nitida
(*Indian Laurel*)
Ficus radicans 'variegata'
(*Variegated Rooting Fig*)
Ficus stricta 'Philippinense'

All are sturdy, tolerant, ornamental tropicals and sub-tropicals that can be used for decorative accent almost anywhere indoors where the light averages 500 foot candles for at least eight hours a day. True, they will survive lower light situations, as low as 50 foot candles, but the foliage will be sparse, and you will lose the lush tree form desired when selecting these rather expensive plants. Changes of environment (with the exception of Ficus 'Doescheri') such as from vendor to home, office or interior landscape will frequently result in heavy leaf drop. This is only a temporary condition. Once the trees become established in about a month, they will leaf out again. Ficus 'Doescheri' is little affected by moves. Foliage is narrower than Ficus elastica variegata with which it may be confused. 'Doescheri' can be grown at cooler temperatures and lower light. Also, when in moderate to strong light, the midrib and leafstalks will turn pink. Ficus diversifolia, a low growing twiggy shrub, is so named because it produces leaves of more than one shape: some are round, others are pointed. The grey overcast webbing on the leaves is normal and not an indication of accumulated dust or dirt. The inedible fruit, green as it arises from axils at the leaf stems, turns pink as it matures. A gem of a house plant, it also is a fine subject for development into an indoor bonsai. Ficus radicans 'variegata' as well as its all green counterpart make a fine basket, shelf or table plant. Easily trained as topiaries, they often take the blue ribbons whenever placed in competition. Another fine, creeping fig is Ficus pumila commonly known as Ficus repens. A fine plant for baskets, etc., it is best known for its climbing habits, both indoors and outdoors in the South where it is often used in place of ivy as a ground and wall cover. A famous display of this plant may be seen covering the upright columns in the conservatory at Longwood Gardens, Kennett Square, Pa. This plant has one inch long, dark green, heart-shaped leaves. It clings to walls by its roots, in the same manner as ivy. Growing medium for all plants should consist of one part peatmoss to one part potting soil. They prefer to have their roots confined, so don't be in a rush to shift them to larger pots. Water thoroughly when dipstick measures moist three quarters up from the bottom. If the growing pot is set into a larger decorator pot, place bricks on gravel at the bottom and set the growing pot on these. Over watering, or standing water that does not rise high enough to keep the roots constantly wet will not have to be removed.

Maranta leuconeura erythroneura
(Red-veined Prayer Plant)

Maranta leuconeura kerchoveana
(Prayer Plant)

Calathea makoyana
(Peacock Plant)

Maranta
(Prayer Plants)

So named for their folding of leaves in prayer at sunset. This occurs even when there is artificial light in their growing environment.

Maranta leuconeura erythroneura
(Red-veined Prayer Plant)

Maranta leuconeura kerchoveana
(Prayer Plant)

Calathea makoyana
(Peacock Plant)

All have attractive, colorful foliage and interesting form with a low spreading habit. They provide a welcome accent for home or office where they adapt well. Calathea makoyana "peacock plant" has a more erect habit (not much more so) with thin, glossy, parchment feeling foliage. The Marantas make fine plants for basket culture, in low shallow, panlike containers, or even as border plants in a well-lighted room divider. East and west windows are fine providing the sun's rays are diffused most of the time. Direct exposure to sun is not harmful providing such episodes are infrequent. Well-established plants frequently grow tiny orchid blossoms which offer a welcome relief to the all foliage planting. Growing medium should consist of one part peatmoss to one part potting soil. Water thoroughly when dipstick measures moist two thirds up from the bottom.

Nephrolepis
(Boston Fern)

Nephrolepis exaltata bostoniensis
(Boston Fern)

Nephrolepis exaltata bostoniensis compacta
(Dwarf Boston Fern)

Nephrolepis exaltata 'Fluffy Ruffles'
(Dwarf Feather Fern)

Nephrolepis exaltata 'Norwoodii'
(Norwood Lace Fern)

Nephrolepis exaltata 'Whitmanii'
(Whitman Lace Fern)

These are the most adaptable of the decorative ferns currently available. They will tolerate the average home environment and are grown satisfactorily as floor plants, shelf plants and in hanging baskets. Semishade is their preference, but occasional exposure to direct sun for short periods is not harmful. They thrive best where the humidity is somewhat above normal and temperatures vary between 55 and 65 degrees F. Frequent misting and/or a warm gentle shower helps to keep the foliage clean and turgid. A good growing medium is one part peatmoss to one part potting soil. Water when dipstick is moist three quarters up from the bottom.

Nephrolepis exaltata bostoniensis compacta
(*Dwarf Boston Fern*)

Nephrolepis exaltata 'Fluffy Ruffles'
(*Dwarf Feather Fern*)

Nephrolepis exaltata bostoniensis
(*Boston Fern*)

Nephrolepis exaltata 'Norwoodii'
(*Norwood Lace Fern*)

Nephrolepis exaltata 'Whitmanii'
(*Whitman Lace Fern*)

Peperomia obtusifolia 'variegata'
(Variegated Peperomia)

Peperomia caperata
(Emerald Ripple)

Peperomia caperata
(Emerald Ripple)

Peperomia obtusifolia
(Baby Rubber Plant)

Peperomia obtusifolia 'variegata'
(Variegated Peperomia)

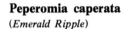

Small, decorative foliage plants with low, bushy growing habits that make them ideally suited for dish gardens, small desk or shelf plants. Adaptable to average interior atmospheres and humidity, they will tolerate heavy traffic and some neglect. Potting soil should consist of one part peatmoss to two parts potting soil. Water only when the soil is bone dry or when the dipstick measures moist only one quarter up from the bottom.

Peperomia obtusifolia
(Baby Rubber Plant)

Phoenix roebelinii
(Dwarf Date Palm)

A popular decorator plant for home use, it softens and accents to best advantage most any situation. A tolerant, robust plant, it will survive in light as low as 20 foot candles but performs better in diffused light of 100 foot candles or more. This exceedingly slow grower will eventually attain a height of 12 feet if conditions are right. Young seedlings are often available in 3-4 inch pots. These make excellent plants for table and shelf culture. Occasional misting or a warm gentle shower helps to keep the foliage clean and bright. Potting soil should consist of one part peatmoss to one part potting soil. Water when dipstick measures moist two thirds up from the bottom. As a high humidity lover, the plant responds well to bathroom culture.

Phoenix roebelinii
(Dwarf Date Palm)

Pilea cadierei
(Aluminum Plant)

Pilea 'Silvertree'
(Silver & Bronze)

Pilea involucrata (Panimiga)
(Friendship Plant)

Pilea 'Moon Valley'

lea 'Moon Valley'

lea cadierei
(uminum Plant)

lea involucrata (Panimiga)
riendship Plant)

lea 'Silvertree'
ilver & Bronze)

Grown in dish gardens, planters or in small pots, these are sturdy adaptables most suited to home culture, even though they often are found to thrive as personal desk plants in large offices. Although this group of plants prefers to grow in strong dif-fused light, they can survive a lower light level if occasionally moved to areas where light is intense. Potting soil should consist one part peatmoss to one part potting soil. Water thoroughly when dipstick reads moist one half way up from the bottom.

Platycerium diversifolium
(Erect Elkhorn)

So named because of their diverse frond forms that are widely different in shape and color. The flat, rounded, tan parchment-like shield encloses the roots and clasps to its growing support such as bark or osmunda fiber. The antler-like grey-green fuzz on fronds grow from the center of the shield. These attractive tropicals like to be kept moist at all times and are best kept in kitchen or bathroom where watering can easily be accomplished on

Platycerium diversifolium
(Erect Elkhorn)

Plectranthus australis
(Swedish Ivy)

a daily basis. Plant and growing medium should be thoroughly soaked with water to which fish emulsion has

been added at a rate of one cap per gallon. Water misting with fish emulsion solution is another means of maintaining these plants.

Plectranthus australis
(Swedish Ivy)

A gem of a plant for basket culture or as a pot plant that cascades vigorously over a shelf. Adaptable to the average indoor environment, it will tolerate heavy traffic and occasional neglect. It is frequently used as a living window curtain when lush baskets hung at different levels permit a modicum of

Polypodium aureum 'Mandaianum'
(Crisped Blue Fern)

privacy without having to cover the glass. Grown in a temperature range of 55-70 degrees plus occasional water misting, the plant will perform well. A suitable soil medium consists of one part peatmoss to one part potting soil. The dipstick should read moist half way up from the bottom before further watering is required.

Polypodium aureum 'Mandaianum'
(Crisped Blue Fern)

Another fine decorator fern that can be grown as a floor or table plant, within a compatible indoor landscape, or in a hanging basket. Texture and form are different from most ferns. Its

large segmented bluish fronds ar growing habit make a striking acce wherever the plant is used. Adaptab to the average indoor environment, will tolerate a wide variation of ten perature and light as low as 50 fo candles. Although exposure to dire sunlight at short intervals is benefici for maintaining its blue-green color, diffused light location is best f growth. Frequent misting keeps fron clean and crisp. A suitable growin medium is one part peatmoss to on part potting soil. Water thorough! when the dipstick reads moist tw thirds up from the bottom.

Polyscias balfouriana marginata
(Variegated Balfouriana)

Polyscias balfouriana marginata
(*Variegated Balfouriana*)

This is the variegated form of Polyscias balfouriana. Both have same form and growing habit. A tropical tree-like shrub, it adapts well for use as a decorative plant in the home environment. Although mostly available as large tub specimens, they are frequently available in sizes small enough for use as table or plant stand subjects. Until acclimated expect considerable leaf fall. They prefer to grow in diffused light rather than in the sun and will tolerate light as low as 100 foot candles. A good growing medium is a one-to-one mix of peatmoss and potting soil. Water thoroughly when dipstick shows moist three quarters up from the bottom.

Pseudorhipsalis macrantha
(*Fragrant Moondrops*)

This is a tree-climbing cactus that adapts readily to home culture. In its apparent ugliness, it becomes a thing of beauty when grown in a hanging basket or as a trailing shelf plant where its jade green scalloped, succulent flat strap-like form makes a welcome relief from the usual foliage plants associated with baskets. A fine window

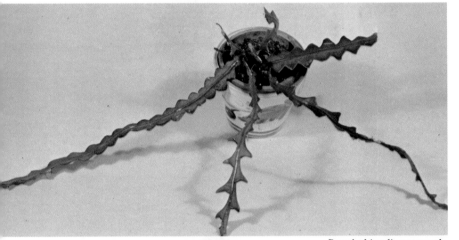

Pseudorhipsalis macrantha
(*Fragrant Moondrops*)

Pteris cretica 'Wimsettii'
(*Skeleton Table Fern*)

plant, it tolerates the dry warm atmosphere of our homes and will survive occasional neglect. Too much direct sunlight will sunburn this highly decorative plant. When in bloom it fills the air with a refreshing lemony fragrance. The growing medium should consist of one part peatmoss to one part cactus potting soil. Water only when the dipstick is moist one quarter up from the bottom.

Pteris cretica 'Wimsettii'
(*Skeleton Table Fern*)

This variety is the most robust of the table ferns. It will tolerate chilling, neglectful watering and a wide range of light intensities. Rarely exceeding a height of 18 inches, it makes an interesting subject for a dining room table centerpiece as well as a fine shelf or sill plant. It also may be used for decorative accent in terrariums, dish gardens, filler for planters, as ground cover for a large tubbed plant or even as a low floor plant since it is sturdy enough to take heavy traffic and occasional drafts. Growing medium should consist of one part potting soil to one part peatmoss. Water feed with fish emulsion at the rate of one cap of emulsion to two quarts of water, when the dipstick reads moist two thirds up from the bottom.

Rhapsis excelsa (Flabelliformis)
(*Lady Palm*)

Grown in dense clumps of slender, erect cane-like stems with fan formed foliage, this plant makes an exquisite tubbed specimen that rarely exceeds 12 feet in height. It performs satisfactorily in average warm, arid indoor atmospheres and in light 100 foot candles and above. A decorative accent plant for the home, it should be given time to establish itself in its permanent setting. Frequent moves hurt the plant's performance. A one to one mix of soil and peatmoss serves as a good growing medium. Water when dipstick reads moist one half way up from the bottom. When new growth commences, a water/feed program should begin. One cap of fish emulsion should be added to each two quarts of water for growth to be maximized.

Rhoeo spathacea (discolor)
(Moses-in-the-Cradle)

Rhoeo spathacea (discolor)
(Moses-in-the-Cradle)

A superior, colorful, low growing foliage plant for window sill culture or in planters where light intensity averages 200 foot candles. The 8-12 inch lance-shaped velvety green leaves are undercoated in rich purple. Rosettes contain shell-like bracts (cradles) arising from leaf axils. Small white flowers appear to be resting in the bracts. The unusual arrangement of bracts and flowers is responsible for the common name "Moses-in-the-cradle." Growth is best accomplished in a one to one mix of peatmoss and potting soil. Water when dipstick reads moist one third up from the bottom.

Rubus reflexus
(Trailing Velvet Plant)

A sturdy, attractive trailing plant that prefers a warm, humid environment, yet will adapt to conditions less than optimum. Fine as a basket or trailing shelf plant, it also can be trained to frame a window or grow on trellis. Water thoroughly when dipstick reads moist half way up from the bottom. Potting soil and peatmoss mixed in equal amounts, promote good growth.

Tradescantia flumensis 'variegata'
(Variegated Wandering Jew)

Tradescantia multiflora
(Tahitian Bridal Veil)

Tradescantia Zebrina pendula 'quadricolor'
(Gay Wandering Jew)

All of the genus Commelinaceae these "inch plants," (so named because

Tradescantia Zebrina pendula 'quadricolor'
(Gay Wandering Jew)

Tradescantia flumensis 'variegata'
(Variegated Wandering Jew)

Tradescantia multiflora
(Tahitian Bridal Veil)

the distance between nodes) can be
~wn in pots, as trailing shelf
ieties, window sill subjects or in
aging baskets. Each is adaptable,
ractive and gay. Ideally, they prefer
ong light with a dash of dappled
llight part of the day, yet will grow
rly well in light of just 100 foot
ndles. It's easy to break off pieces
en handling, yet equally simple to
nt these parts and start new plants,
viding a node is present. Pieces also
be rooted in water. A suitable
wing medium is one part peatmoss
two parts potting soil. Water when
stick measures moist one half way
from the bottom.

Saintpaulia (*African Violet*)

A universally-favored easy-to-grow
houseplant, the African violets of today
have been bred for durability, year-
round flowering and attractive foliage.
They have come a long way from the
small, single, purple-flowered native
African species that were first introduced to indoor gardeners at the
turn of the century. Typical of the new
breed of African violets are the
'Rhapsodie' hybrids such as "Gisela"
and "Ophelia" with their free
flowering robust habit. Another
development has been the breeding of
variegated flowering plants such as
"Firebird." Grown in a collection or

singly as table or sill plant, African
violets prefer the kind of light normally
found in front of a draft-free, unobstructed east window during the
shorter days of fall on through the
winter to early spring. As the days
lengthen and the sun gets stronger, it is
best to move plants one pot width back
into the room or to depend upon
overhanging tree branches as light
filters. African violets have distinct
preferences for light. Varieties such as
"Snow Ballet," with its foliage stret-
ching up and out to the light, indicates
that greater light intensity is required.
"Lullaby," growing in the same
window, curls its leaves close to the pot,

Saintpaulia 'Gisela'

Saintpaulia 'Ophelia'

Saintpaulia 'Firebird'

Saintpaulia 'Snow Ballet'

attempting to escape. Apparently the light is too strong for this variety. In each case a change of position on the window would help. Most plants, however, will adapt to mild fluctuations of temperature, but prefer a much higher than normal humidity than normally found in the home. Temperatures can range from 60 to 80 degrees F. without the need to increase air circulation. African violets do best if they have a continuous source of moisture and food. To satisfy this demand, pots can be equipped with a piece of aluminum mesh placed inside over the drainage holes. Through this is drawn a thin strip of nylon stocking. This serves as an umbilical cord to the feed/water container. A margarine container with a hole cut into its top makes an ideal source cup. The potted plant rests on the plastic cover, thereby avoiding all contact with the solution, other than through the nylon stocking. Although African violets need repotting, this can be delayed by cutting out the center of a plastic container cover and slipping it under the plant's leaves in the same manner as for a collar. Additional humidity can be added through the introduction of small open trays of water placed nearby. Water misting with luke warm water twice a day also prevents dehydration. Because of the continuous water-feed system utilized to keep these plants in peak condition, a water soluble fertilizer must be employed. It is suggested that only one quarter of the amount recommended on the package be used. Alternation between three or four kinds, utilizing a different one each week, also is desirable. A suitable rotation may be fish emulsion during the first week, Hyponex, the second, Miracid, third, and Peter's, fourth. This gives the plants a good mix of organic and chemical nutrients along with trace elements. If repotting is necessary, use a mix of one part vermiculite to one part chopped sphagnum peatmoss and one part prepared potting soil formulated for African violets.

Saintpaulia 'Lullaby'

Saintpaulia 'Grenadier'

Saintpaulia 'Top Dollar'

Plants classified in this section as requiring full light should receive direct sunlight at least 50 percent of the daylight hours.

1000 or More Footcandles

This is the unobstructed bright light t is found in front of windows that ve southern or western exposure. It o can be described as the kind of inse light normally associated with shaded greenhouses, window greenuses and garden rooms. Full light is timum for the growing and ooming of most plants other than the ade lovers such as Helxine soleirolii aby's Tears" or Selaginella "Sweat nt."

Although this light is fine for pot ants during the shorter, often cloudy ys of fall, winter and early spring; ecautions against plant sunburn, eaching and heat buildup must be ken during late spring and summer en the days are long and light inteny reaches 3000 or more foot candles.

Plants growing in the wild make adstments. Yet, these same plants conned to pots cannot adapt and often nd up as sad drooping desiccated ecimens with cooked roots.

Greenhouse, garden room and ndow greenhouse growers shade eir windows during this time of year d so can you. Wood slat blinds, glass rtains or bamboo shades not only eak the light during the period when ht is most intense, but also act as inators against heavy heat buildup.

Greenhouse growers vent the owing areas to prevent "cooking." is also should be done by the houseanter by opening windows and tering more frequently.

To avoid sunburn or actual leaf orch, move the plants into the room m the glass so they do not touch it. so, do this in winter to prevent liage freeze against the glass when e temperatures drop below freezing.

REENHOUSES

The best method of providing optium growing light for indoor garning is, of course, a free standing eenhouse. This is where plants are forded unobstructed light on all sides d overhead from dawn to dusk.

Even in this kind of environment it is st to grow compatible plants, since

basically, you can only recreate and maintain the heat and humidity typical of one native habitat. In this kind of situation, light is not the primary factor since even in a greenhouse, there are different light zones.

Plan your collection so that low light plants are grown under benches and on the floor.

Those plants liking moderate amounts of sun should be placed on benches, and sun lovers can be set on shelves suspended over the benches or even hung on wire from the top ridge.

WINDOW GREENHOUSES

If the feasibility of a greenhouse is in question, you can still increase fulllight growing space with the installation of a window greenhouse. These come in many different sizes and can be made to fit any double-hung window.

To gain the greatest amount of available light, adjustable wire mesh shelves are used. Overhead glass also serves as a light source in addition to providing ventilation.

The bottom shelf is lined with a sheet metal tray that holds water and pebbles. Pots of moisture loving plants are set on the pebble-laden tray to take advantage of the humidity. Each plant should be set on its own saucer so dripping from high to low shelves is avoided.

ARTIFICIAL LIGHT

You can grow and bloom plants indoors without the natural, bright foot candles of sunlight that most plants require. Since the development of fluorescent "grow" lamps that incorporate nearly all portions of the color spectrum, natural sunlight is imitated. These units can be placed anywhere in the home or office.

For best results, plants grown under these lights require a "day" of 12-14 hours. Frequency of watering and feeding will need to be increased for plants raised under these conditions, because they never rest. Under natural conditions an occasional overcast day will slow growth rate, thus decreasing the need for plant food and water.

Agave victoria-reginae
(*Queen Agave*)
Agave attenuata
(*Tree Agave*)

These are slow growing succulents that adapt well to the home or work atmosphere. Tolerant of abuse, low or high temperatures, drafts and light as low as 100 foot candles, they manage to survive even under the most adverse conditions. A planting of agave in a desert landscape within an office building has survived for six years. Water only when the soil is bone dry or when the dipstick is barely damp one quarter up from the bottom. These plants prefer to have their roots confined. Therefore, only repot them when the container can no longer restrict their growth. The best potting medium consists of one part parakeet gravel to two parts specialty cactus potting soil.

Abutilon striatum 'aureomaculatum'
(*Flowering Maple*)

For year-round bloom and to maintain its compact, shrubby habit, this adaptable window sill plant prefers placement in an unobstructed, sunny location that receives a minimum of four hours full sunlight in winter and larger amounts during summer months. It also can be kept blooming freely if grown under an artificial light unit, where the grow lamps provide intensity of 1000 foot candles for 14 hours a day. Note in the illustratic that half of the plant's foliage variegated, while the remainder is so green. This is not caused by "sporting (genetic change), but by a no contagious virus that naturally occu on this variety. Water thoroughly wh dipstick reads moist one third fro the bottom. The growing mediu should consist of one part peatmoss one part potting soil.

Ardisia crispa (Crenulata)

This is a tropical holly-like evergre that produces red berries just like northern cousins. Ranging in heig from 2-4 feet, these trees adapt well average indoor growing conditions a

Abutilon striatum 'aureomaculatum'
(*Flowering Maple*)
Agave victoria-reginae
(*Queen Agave*)

Agave attenuata
(*Tree Agave*)

will hold their colorful fruit for about six months of the year. These decorative, graceful plants make excellent floor or table subjects. Small seedlings are often used in a mixed planting of compatible greens or as sill or shelf plants. They perform best in a west window where there is sunlight four or more hours during the winter and nearly all day during summer months, providing pots are moved back from the window 4-6 inches. Temperature preference ranges from 50-60 degrees F. and humidity should measure 30 per cent. Frequent misting, pebble tray culture as well as double potting all help to increase humidity around the plants. Water thoroughly each time the dipstick reads three quarters up from the bottom. A suitable medium should consist of one part peatmoss to one part potting soil.

Araucaria bidwillii
(*Monkey Puzzle*)
Araucaria excelsa
(*Norfolk Island Pine*)

These are tropical and subtropical evergreen conifers with typical pyramidal form; pine needle-like foliage and resinous fragrant sap. Normally available in sizes two feet or more in pots, smaller plants also are marketed. The small plants can be grown quite rapidly for eventual seasonal use as Christmas trees, when not serving their initial purpose as decorative accent plants. Even the small plants may serve this dual purpose. Culturally, these plants prefer a cool, bright situation, but will adapt quite satisfactorily to the average interior environment. Exceptionally durable, they are not temperamental and may be used successfully where there is good light and good air circulation. Too much or too little light will be indicated by heavy needle fall. Just move the plant to a better location and it will recuperate. If you are satisfied with the size of the plant, keep it root bound as long as possible before shifting it to a larger container or else it may outgrow your home. Given the root space, they can grow as high as the roof allows. Outside, these plants attain a height of 200 or more feet. Water thoroughly when dipstick reads moist three quarters up from the bottom. Growing medium should consist of one part peatmoss to two parts potting soil.

Araucaria bidwillii
(*Monkey Puzzle*)

Araucaria excelsa
(*Norfolk Island Pine*)

Ardisia crispa (Crenulata)

Beaucarnea recurvata (*Nolina*)
(*Bottle Palm*)

Begonia semperflorens
(*Wax Begonia*)

Beaucarnea recurvata (Nolina)
(*Bottle Palm*)

Reaching 30 feet in height where native, these attractive decorative succulents may be used in any indoor situation that can be enhanced by the character and free-spirited growth habit of this durable pot plant. They adapt satisfactorily to the average indoor warm, arid atmosphere, tolerate abuse and an occasional drought. The frequent vacationer finds these plants extremely cooperative. Some have been known to survive a year without water, in their native habitat, living off stored moisture in their bulbous bases. A full sun situation is their preference, yet they will survive in light as low as 100 foot candles. This plant can be grown as an indoor bonsai. Although it retains all of its characteristics, the dwarfing process causes the balloon-like base to flatten because of confinement in small low containers. Water only when bone dry or when dipstick indicates damp one quarter up from the bottom. An adequate growing mix consists of one part peatmoss to two parts specialty cactus potting soil.

Begonia semperflorens
(*Wax Begonia*)

Widely used outdoors in annual beds, borders and planters, the fibrous-rooted begonia is also grown extensively indoors wherever there is sufficient light and humidity. They prefer cool nights, down to 55 degrees and warm days of up to 75 degrees F. but will adapt to other than perfect temperatures. Light and humidity are the keys to good health. They will thrive on a south or west window in the full sun of winter, yet require some shading during the intense heat and strong sun of summer. Since they prefer a minimum of 30 per cent humidity to maintain their glossy, green succulent foliage in prime condition and free blooming habit, pebble tray culture or its equivalent should be used. Insufficient light is usually indicated by leggy, one sided growth and sparse flowering. Dry margins around the leaves and heavy loss of foliage is a sure sign that humidity must be increased. Leaf drop may also be caused by poor watering practices. Although these plants enjoy a humid atmosphere, the soil must be permitted to go almost dry between each thorough watering. Water only when dipstick reads damp one third up from the bottom of the pot. Growth is best achieved in a medium of one part potting soil to one part peatmoss.

Echinocactus grusonii

Mammilaria compressa
(Mother of Hundreds)

Notocactus leninghausii
(Golden Ball)

Opuntia rufida
(Cinnamon Cactus)

Cephalocereus senilis
(Old Man Cactus)

Opuntia vestita
(Cotton-Pole)

Opuntia microdasys
(Bunny Ears)

Cactus

Cacti are spiny or thorned succulents without leaves or in some instances having vestigial leaves. All are native to the hot, arid sections of the western hemisphere where rainfall is at a minimum. Having evolved into natural water storage tanks with waxy skin that prevents rapid transpiration, these plants have been known to survive without additional water year to year, depending only on spring showers. Minimum care plants, they actually thrive in the average dry indoor environment. They are little affected by temperature fluctuations, yet do prefer readings of 55 degrees F. and above. Watering should be restrained. Only water thoroughly when the soil is bone dry and no dampness is indicated on the dip stick. Cacti come in many forms, shapes and sizes. The following

are just a few of the many varieties that are available commercially:

Echinocactus grusonii
(Golden Barrel)

Mammilaria compressa
(Mother of Hundreds)

Notocactus leninghausii
(Golden Ball)

Opuntia vestita
(Cotton-Pole)

Cephalocereus senilis
(Old Man Cactus)

Opuntia microdasys
(Bunny Ears)

Opuntia rufida
(Cinnamon Cactus)

Grafting of certain cacti to sturdy understock such as Hylocereus guatemalensis or Cereus peruvianus has long been practiced to speed growth of slow specimens; to preserve and protect tender varieties; or in the case of recent introductions of mutation grafts from Japan, provide a source of chlorophyll. If offshoots should form at the base of hylocereus, remove them to avoid competition to the rest of the plant. If this occurs in the Japanese imports, leave them alone because these offshoots will eventually perish.

Chlorophytum comosum 'Vittatum'
(Spider Plant)

Chlorophytum comosum 'Vittatum'
(Spider Plant)

These are sturdy, adaptable, minimum care plants that will tolerate occasional abuse. Although they will survive in light as poor as 100 foot candles, light from an unobstructed south or west window during the shorter days of the year and partial shading during the remainder is preferred. They're fine plants for growing in the home or at work. Large and small varieties make attractive basket plants with their sword shaped variegated foliage and plantlets trailing over the pot's rim. Shelf or table locations also work well. Water thoroughly only when the dipstick measures one third damp up from the bottom. An occasional shower in the sink and/or water misting help to keep the foliage bright and decorative. A suitable potting medium is a 50-50 mix of peatmoss and potting soil.

Coccoloba uvifera
(Sea Grape)

Native to the sandy, tropical shores of Florida and the West Indies, this plant adapts well to most any indoor situation at home or at work. A robust shrub-like tree, it can be used effec-

Coccoloba uvifera
(Sea Grape)

tively as a single, free-standing specimen or as the central figure within a group. The average height is 3-5 feet, while width is nearly the same. In the wild, however, this plant often attains a height of 20 feet or more. A natural lover of full sunlight, it also will survive in light as low as 50 foot candles. Water thoroughly when dipstick reads three quarters moist from the bottom. Equal amounts of peatmoss and potting soil, mixed together, make an ideal potting soil for this plant.

Codiaeum 'Gloriosum superbum'
(Autumn Croton)
Codiaeum 'Norwood Beauty'
(Oakleaf Croton)

Codiaeum 'L. M. Rutherford'
(Giant Croton)

Wherever these plants are placed, a gay, decorative mood is introduced, primarily because of colorful foliage with varietal forms. Tolerant of mo indoor atmospheres, they are happie in a warm, humid situation, and ada best whenever the moisture percenta is 30. Strong light intensifies colors the leaves as they mature. Yet, they require some shading during t brightest days of summer. Sma young plants are frequently included compatible dish gardens. Larg specimens may be used on wind sills, shelves, tables, on the floor or interior landscapes. Since these plan do prefer a warm humid atmospher pebble culture and/or double potti will offer best success. Water when t dipstick reads moist three quarte from the bottom. An ideal potting m is one part peatmoss to one pa potting soil.

Codiaeum 'L. M. Rutherford'
(Giant Croton)

Codiaeum 'Norwood Beauty'
(Oakleaf Croton)

Codiaeum 'Gloriosum superbum'
(Autumn Croton)

Coffea arabica
(Arabian Coffee)

Coffea arabica
(Arabian Coffee)

This elegant evergreen shrub has adapted so well to our indoor environments that it has become one of the favorite plants of homeowners, interior decorators, florists and landscapers. Small plants are fine for sills, shelves, and tables while larger, tubbed specimens make superior floor plants that will tolerate heavy traffic and occasional neglect. Proper lighting is the key to these plants' health. Unobstructed south or west window light from late fall to mid-spring and some shading thereafter will keep the plant airy, compact and shrubby. Coffea arabica will tolerate light as low as 100 foot candles, but leaf drop will be heavy. Water when dipstick is moist two thirds up from the bottom. Equal amounts of peatmoss and potting soil in a mix will provide an adequate soil medium.

Coleus
(*Painted Nettle*)

Grown for their brightly-colored foliage and their varied forms, coleus adapt well to the average indoor environment at home or at work. Often used as bedding or border plants, they perform satisfactorily on any bright window and make excellent subjects for artificial light culture. Insufficient light decreases the size and color in-

100 foot candles, performance increases as the light gets stronger. Water when the dipstick reads moist one half way up from the bottom. An occasional shower and/or warm water misting will keep foliage clean. Grow in a mix of one part peatmoss and one part potting soil.

Coleus
(*Painted Nettle*)

Erybotrya japonica
(*Chinese Loquat*)

tensity of their foliage. It also encourages weak, leggy growth. Once they take hold, growth is rapid. Their growing tips should be pinched to keep them bushy and within bounds. Flower buds should be removed before opening to insure colorful, lush foliage. Shading may be necessary during the bright hot days of summer. Water when dipstick reads moist three fourths up from the bottom. A suitable growing mix is one part peatmoss to two parts potting soil.

Dizygotheca elegantissima
(*Spider Aralia*)

Graceful, airy, and delicate in appearance, this sturdy gay deceiver can be used to decorate any interior. The plant is available in sizes from 2 1/4-inch pot plants to magnificent tubbed specimens. Adaptable to most bright light situations, some shading and venting will be required during the long bright, hot days of summer. Although they will tolerate light of just

Dizygotheca elegantissima
(*Spider Aralia*)

Erybotrya japonica
(*Chinese Loquat*)

An elegant, sturdy, decorative evergreen tree that carries its formal symmetrical head on an erect trunk. Adaptable to average indoor environments, it performs best in sunny, yet cool locations. An economic plant, it will flower and fruit if growing conditions are correct. Water when dipstick reads moist three quarters up from the bottom. A suitable potting mix is one part peatmoss to one part potting soil.

Euphorbia splendens
(*Crown of Thorns*)

Euphorbia splendens bojeri
(*Dwarf Crown of Thorns*)

A sturdy plant for warm sunny locations at home or at work. Because it rarely needs shading, it works well in desert gardens, compatible dish gardens or even in individual pots. Young wood is soft enough for training to stakes. The stakes can be used for omoting erect growth or when placed round the pot's perimeter, encouraging a truly spiny crown. The sturdy euphorbia splendens bojeri, because of s small foliage and growing habit, can asily be trained as a bonsai. Do not be scouraged, if in the late fall and inter, foliage turns yellow and considerable leaf drop occurs. This is ormal. When days lengthen and the n gets stronger, plants leaf out and

environments, light is the key to top performance, even though these plants are known to survive in light as poor as 20 foot candles. Almost succulent in nature, with foliage coated with a natural wax, ficus elastica "Decora" will require little or no shading. Water when dipstick is moist one third up from the bottom. A suitable growing medium is one part potting soil to one part peatmoss.

Ficus elastica 'Decora'
(Rubber Plant)

Euphorbia splendens   *Euphorbia splendens bojeri*
(Crown of Thorns)   *(Dwarf Crown of Thorns)*

bloom. Water logged soil encourages oot rot in these plants, so let it go almost completely dry between aterings. Water only when dipstick is amp one quarter up from the bottom. A good planting medium should consist of one part peatmoss to two parts potting soil for cactus.

Ficus elastica 'Decora'
(Rubber Plant)

A favorite decorator tree used wherever its large, green glossy leaves and robust spreading form can serve as a frame for any window. Specimen plants in heights from 2-4 feet, when placed in good light, will soon catch up to the tall, expensive plants. Typical of many tropical trees, these sprout aerial roots that grow into the soil to form additional trunks. If a single, strong trunk is desired, remove these roots as they appear. Adaptable to most indoor

Gynura sarmentosa
(Velvet Plant)

A gem of a plant for window sill, shelf or hanging basket. Without having to depend on bloom, it works well with a compatible collection of coleus or geraniums to provide striking, attractive color year-round. To keep the plant compact and bushy, pinch out the growing tips after each formation of new leaves. Leaf spot can be prevented by carefully watering the plant, making certain spray does not touch leaves. The dipstick should read just one half way up from the bottom before watering. A good planting medium is one part peatmoss to one part potting soil.

Gynura sarmentosa
(Velvet Plant)

Black peppermint, spearmint, wooly applemint, marjoram, nutmeg scented thyme, French thyme, lemon scented thyme, and golden thyme were purchased as started pot plants.

HERBS

Through the ages, man has used herbs for medicinal purposes, to scent the air, as food and flavorings, in perfumes and as preservatives. Most herbs are perennials native to the Mediterranean and perform best when grown outdoors. Fortunately for the houseplanter who gardens mostly indoors, certain of the most frequently used cooking herbs can be grown successfully on a bright sunny window sill or in an artificial light garden without taking up too much precious space. Fresh herbs are usually more potent than the dried, so there isn't the need to produce massive specimens to satisfy the needs of an average household. Plants can be maintained in 3 inch pots for more than a year before requiring repotting. A humid microenvironment keeps these plants producing and also cuts down on the need to water. A continually damp pebble or soil bed on which the pots are set provides a humid environment. Although these plants can be grown as attractive individual specimens in decorator pots or hanging baskets, treatment as food plants is the most appropriate. Water when dipstick reads moist half way up from the bottom. An appropriate medium is one part peatmoss to two parts potting soil.

Grown from a cutting is Pelargonium 'Prince Ruppert variegated' "Lemon scented geranium." An excellent plant for flavoring and scenting.

Curly parsley, chives at different stages of growth after snipping, and a jaffa orange seedling were all started from seed.

Petroselimum crispum "Parsley" is a very compact, dark-green heavy-flavored plant. This specimen was started from seed.

...smarinus officinalis "Rosemary" is used for ...vorings, in medicines and perfume. It also is ...rted from seed.

Hoya carnosa
(*Wax Plant*)

Hoya carnosa variega
(*Variegated Wax Plaи*)

Hoya carnosa compac
(*Hindu Rope*)

Hoya carnosa
(*Wax Plant*)

Hoya carnosa variegata
(*Variegated Wax Plant*)

Hoya carnosa compacta
(*Hindu Rope*)

Sturdy, robust climbers, these plants love the strong full sun of west windows. In fact, coloration increases as light intensity builds. Tolerant of most indoor environments, they will adapt to dryness even though they prefer a humid atmosphere. Most frequently available as basket subjects and small pot plants, they can be used effectively wherever the light is strong and bright. They train easily to trellis and wire. The waxy fragrant flowers, borne on spurs, should never be removed after they have passed their prime because buds for succeeding blooms also are formed on the spurs. Water when dipstick reads moist half way up from the bottom. A one to one mix of peatmoss and potting soil will provide a suitable growing medium.

sine herbstii 'aureoreticulata'
(icken Gizzard)

A tropical perennial herb that has
pted to indoor culture and environ-
nts. Erect in habit to one foot tall,
colorful foliage and red stems add
come color to any window sill or
t garden collection. Since their re-
irements are about the same, these
can be included with geraniums,
eus and begonias. Water when dipstick reads moist one half way up from
the bottom. A suitable potting mix
consists of one part peatmoss to one
part potting soil. To keep this plant
bushy and compact, pinch out growing
tips as deemed necessary.

Kalanchoe blossfeldiana 'compacta'
(Christmas Kalanchoe)
Kalanchoe fedtschenkoi 'marginata'
(Rainbow Kalanchoe)

Ligustrum lucidum
(Glossy Privet)

from the bottom. A suggested soil mix
is one part peatmoss to two parts
potting soil.

Ligustrum lucidum
(Glossy Privet)

When available as large tubbed
specimens, these plants cannot be
matched for their performance and decorative value in the home or at work.
Tolerant of fluctuating temperatures
and average indoor atmosphere, even
though they prefer full sun, they will
survive in light readings of 50 foot
candles or more. Small plants are often
used in dish gardens while the large
ones are used as floor specimens, or in
indoor landscapes. Heavy feeders, they
must be fed each time watering takes
place. Because water is essential to this
plant's health, thoroughly soak when
the dipstick reads three quarters up
from the bottom. Provide a soil mix of
one part peatmoss to one part potting
soil for best results.

Iresine herbstii 'aureoreticulata'
(Chicken Gizzard)

Kalanchoe fedtschenkoi 'marginata'
(Rainbow Kalanchoe)

Kalanchoe pumila violet
(Dwarf Violet Kalanchoe)
Kalanchoe blossfeldiana 'compacta'
(Christmas Kalanchoe)
Kalanchoe pumila red
(Dwarf Red Kalanchoe)

Kalanchoe pumila red
(Dwarf Red Kalanchoe)
Kalanchoe pumila violet
(Dwarf Violet Kalanchoe)

Short shrubby, compact succulents,
these attractive plants show off their
blooms from early winter to mid-
spring. Easy to care for plants, they tolerate average indoor environments,
and work well in dish gardens, compatible gardens or as specimens.
They're useful as decorative accents
even when blooming has ceased.
Blooming period can be extended if
plants are placed in bright light or
where red incandescent bulbs (40 watt)
burn 10-12 hours a day. Water only
when dipstick reads moist one third up

Lithops turbiniformis
(*Living Stones*)

Lithops turbiniformis
(*Living Stones*)

Not the easiest of plants to manage, they have been included because of their availability and to help you avoid the pitfalls usually encountered by those persons attempting to grow this curiosity. Mimics of their environment, they have evolved to their present form as a means of protection and preservation. They are desert plants, and as such, seek shelter from the elements by growing underground. Sufficient surface is exposed, however, to receive sunlight. Short-lived daisy-like blooms equalling or larger in size than the plant appear in late fall. Strong light is the key to efficient growth. Where strong light is not present, plants stretch out of the soil, lose their character and eventually collapse. Watering must be restrained or rotting will occur. Let the soil go bone dry. After a week of zero readings on the dipstick, watering can be accomplished. A suitable soil mix consists of one part parakeet gravel to one part specialty cactus potting soil. Because these plants retain their same size, little or no repotting need occur after the plant has matured.

Oxalis vulcanicola siliquosa

You have a wide variety of these dainty, cloverleaf foliage type plants from which to choose. They can be grown on a sunny window sill or in an artificial light garden. Excellent as basket or pot plants, most are early spring bloomers. According to variety, they have a color range of white, pink, yellow, red, rose and violet flowers. As the days get shorter, some varieties have a tendency to slow down their growth or go completely dormant (defoliate). Do not be discouraged, leave them alone in their regular growing location and they will soon resume leaf and flower production as daylength eventually increases. Blooming and growth can be extended if the plants are grown under artificial light for 12-14 hours a day. Because they're water/humidity sensitive plants, leaves will droop or close when there is an insufficiency. Water only when dipstick is moist three quarters up from the bottom. A mix of one part peatmoss to one part potting soil will serve as a good potting medium.

Pelargonium X Hortorum 'Emma Hossler'
(*Dwarf Geranium*)

This variety is one of a group of superior dwarfs that

Oxalis vulcanicola siliquosa

iginated in Holland and which retain
eir compact, small leaved, shrubby
e blooming habits. Also having these
aracteristics are "Tu-Tone" and
Mr. Everaarts." An unobstructed
st window appears to be the best
ot for them, as they'll often bloom up
til Christmas. Although they are
mewhat tall for the artificial light
rdener, performance is satisfactory if
hts are left on 14-16 hours per day.

argonium X Hortorum
(range-red Geranium)   Garden
rieties that adapt well to indoor
lture. Plants with semi-double to
uble florets hold up best in the
indow garden because they do not
shatter upon fading. Petal fall of the
single varieties is messy and can stain
carpeting and draperies.

Pelargonium peltatum
(*Ivy Geraniums*)   This group includes
the new dwarf introduction "Sugar
Baby," which is a free-blooming,
sturdy, compact plant that finds use in
pot and basket. Its larger relatives,
such as "Sybil Holmes," are very
robust and often grown as ground-
covers in California.

Pelargonium peltatum 'L'elegante'
(*Sunset Ivy*)

An old European variety that has
proven its decorative value and
durability through the years. In-
creasingly strong light and long days
intensify its coloration. Although
grown primarily for its foliage, it does
grow small single white flowers.
Because it is extremely sensitive, let the
dip stick dry out before watering.

Unless otherwise specified, geraniums should be watered only when the
dipstick is moist one third up from the
bottom or if the foliage appears to wilt
two or three days after a thorough
watering. In the hot dry days of
summer, you may find that there is frequent wilting even though the plant
may have been watered within 24
hours. Check the stick first before
dashing for the watering can. This kind
of wilting may be caused by the plant's
loss of water at a faster rate than roots
can draw it in. The best remedy for this
kind of wilt is to move the plant back
from strong light and heat until it
perks up. Contrary to old time
practice, create a light porous growing
medium. Such a mix is one part peatmoss, one part soil and one part parakeet gravel.

Pelargonium X Hortorum 'Emma Hossler'
(Dwarf Geranium)

Pelargonium X Hortorum
(Orange-red Geranium)

Pelargonium peltatum 'Sugar Baby'
Pelargonium peltatum 'L'elegante'
(Sunset Ivy)

75

Pittosporum tobira
(Japanese pittosporum)

Robust and durable, grandiflora varieties have been hybridized for vigorous, cascading habits, large flowers, and prolific blooming.

Petunia X hybrida grandiflora 'Pink Cascade'

Robust and durable, these varieties have been hybridized by Pan America Seed Co. for their compact, cascading, large flowered, free blooming habits. Prone to winterkill when grown outdoors in the north, this perennial of tropical ancestry can be kept growing and blooming indoors in baskets, pots and planters year-round. They do get a bit leggy and somewhat out of bounds in winter when reaching for light. Judicious pinching helps to keep them in bounds with a minimum loss of flower buds. Wilting may occur during a hot dry spell. Since petunias do not like an overly moist soil or to be moved, shade them and mist before resorting to watering. Before watering is required, the dipstick should read moist half way up from the bottom. A suitable growing medium is one part peatmoss to one part potting soil.

Pittosporum tobira
(Japanese pittosporum)
Pittosporum tobira 'variegatum'
(Variegated Mockorange)

An adaptable, decorative evergreen shrub that performs satisfactorily in the home or at work. Tolerant of most indoor environments and fluctuation of temperatures, it prefers full light, y will manage to survive when just 5 foot candles is present. Excellent as decorative accent or low floor plant, also can be found in small pots for us in dish gardens or as individual s subjects. Water only when dipstick moist one half way up from the bottom Grow them in a mix of one part pea moss to one part potting soil.

Podocarpus macrophylla 'Maki'
(Japanese Yew)

Polyscias fruticosa
(Ming Aralia)

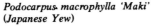

ocarpus macrophylla 'Maki'
anese Yew)

A sturdy decorator plant for floor or erior landscape accent. Its dense, mal habit, spiraling as it grows, ves as a foil for broader-leaved age plants usually used indoors. ailable in large tubbed specimens vn to those in 2 1/4 inch pots, these dled evergreens may be used in npatible dish gardens, on the sill or lf. They take to pruning and ping and are likely candidates for ining as bonsai. A well-rooted speci- n adapts well and can be a thing of uty; whereas a freshly dug and ted up plant runs the risk of weak, r growth or death. Although these

plants prefer a warm sunny location, they will tolerate fluctuating temperatures, heavy traffic and low light to 50 foot candles. Water when dipstick is moist two thirds from the bottom. Grow in a 50-50 mix of peatmoss and potting soil.

Polyscias fruticosa
(Ming Aralia)

A plant for all indoor situations where there is at least 200 foot candles of light. It performs best in the light of a west window that is partially shaded during the hot bright days of summer. Its delicate appearance belies its robust, sturdy character. In its native tropical habitat, it often is used in hedging. There is considerable leaf and

branch drop when placed in a new environment. After a period of adjustment of 3-6 weeks, it will resume growth and regain its vigorous elegant beauty. Fine for bonsai culture because of its knobby wood and growing habit, it is easily trained and maintained. Water when the dipstick reads moist two thirds from the bottom. Equal amounts of potting soil and peatmoss serve as a good soil mix.

Portulacaria afra
Portulacaria afra variegata
(*Rainbow Bush*)

A sturdy, adaptable, long lived small pot plant, it may be grown anywhere there is strong light. Exposure to fluctuating temperatures and arid atmosphere do not appear to affect its health. Some summer shading may be required. Its character of growth, small branches and mini-foliage all lend it to indoor Bonsai culture. Water only when the dipstick is dry. Leaves will begin to shrivel when the plant is desperate for water. Pot in a mix of two parts cactus soil to one part peatmoss.

Rosa chinensis minima
(*Miniature Rose*)

Diminuitive copies of our larger garden roses, these plants are vigorous, durable and adaptable. Ranging in height from 6-12 inches that include a wide variety of forms and colors, they are excellent subjects for window sill and artificial light garden culture. For optimum health and bloom, these plants perform best in a humid, bright, airy, cool environment where the temperature ranges between 55-75 degrees F. Strong sunlight is a must, yet summer shading will be required. Indications of weak growth are the yellowing of foliage and leggy weak growth. Plants set atop damp soil in window boxes or pebbles in water-filled trays should do well. Water when dipstick is damp two thirds up from the bottom. Grow in a mix of one part peatmoss to one part potting soil.

Saxifragae sarmentosa
(*Strawberry Geranium*)

A hardy oriental perennial that has successfully adapted to indoor culture. It can be grown as an individual pot plant, a shelf plant or groundcover; in baskets, compatible dish gardens and terrariums; or trained to a trellis. This plant also likes high humidity, a bright airy environment with temperatures in the 55-75 degree F. range. Humidity can be increased through double potting or water-pebble tray culture.

Portulacaria afr

Portulacaria afra variega
(*Rainbow Bush*)

Rosa chinensis minim
(*Miniature Rose*)

Saxifragae sarmentosa
(*Strawberry Geranium*)

Sedum morganium
(*Burro's Tail*)

Stephanotis floribunda
(*Madagascar Jasmine*)

Strelitzia reginae
(*Bird of Paradise*)

Succulents
(*Kalanchoe, Echeveria, Crassula, Aloe*)

The dipstick should measure damp two thirds up from the bottom. Pot in a 50-50 mix of peatmoss and potting soil.

Stephanotis floribunda
(*Madagascar Jasmine*)

An excellent plant for basket or shelf culture at home or work; this woody stemmed trailer with its attractive dark green thick waxy leaves, adapts most satisfactorily to the average indoor environment. A summer bloomer, it perfumes the air with masses of white, waxy tubular flower clusters. Water when the dipstick is moist two thirds up from the bottom. A suitable potting mix is one part peatmoss to one part potting soil.

Strelitzia reginae
(*Bird of Paradise*)

An adaptable, dramatic, decorative plant in or out of bloom. Rather large of leaf, trunkless and clustering in habit, it is best displayed as a large tub plant. At maturity (three years old) it may grow to 5 feet. A seasonal bloomer from winter to spring, its large, stiff, oblong, grey-green leaves are attractive year-round. Water when the dipstick is moist one half way up from the bottom. Plant in a medium of one part potting soil to one part peatmoss.

Succulents
[*Kalanchoe, Echeveria Crassula, Aloe, Sedum*]

These are a group of plants that have water-filled, fleshy, modified leaves. They do not have needles or spines for protection as do the western hemisphere succulents known as cactus. They do have the capacity to store water because their foliage surface is decreased and coated with wax to prevent excess transpiration. Tolerant of abuse, they adapt satisfactorily to the average arid indoor climate and can be grown in temperatures as low as 50 degrees. Each group has a different character and habit from the other and as such they find use in a variety of situations. Watering should take place only after the dipstick reads dry. A specialty cactus potting soil mixed equally with peatmoss serves as a good growing medium.

Index to Plant Locations